INTRODUCTION

CHAPTER 2: THE PATH TO BECOMING A VIDEO GAME
PROFESSIONAL   7

CHAPTER 3: BUILDING YOUR VIDEO GAME PORTFOLIO   10

CHAPTER 4: MASTERING GAME DESIGN PRINCIPLES   14

CHAPTER 5: PROGRAMMING FUNDAMENTALS FOR VIDEO
GAMES   17

CHAPTER 6: EXPLORING GAME DEVELOPMENT ENGINES 20

CHAPTER 8: INCREASING USER ENGAGEMENT IN ROBLOX
GAMES   27

CHAPTER 9: MONETIZING YOUR ROBLOX GAME   30

CHAPTER 10: UNDERSTANDING USER EXPERIENCE (UX)
DESIGN   33

CHAPTER 11: BUILDING IMMERSIVE VIRTUAL
ENVIRONMENTS   37

CHAPTER 12: IMPLEMENTING 3D GRAPHICS IN VIDEO
GAMES   41

CHAPTER 13: SOUND DESIGN FOR VIDEO GAMES   44

CHAPTER 14: GAME TESTING AND QUALITY ASSURANCE 47

CHAPTER 15: MARKETING STRATEGIES FOR VIDEO GAMES 50

CHAPTER 16: GAME PUBLISHING AND DISTRIBUTION 54

CHAPTER 17: ESPORTS AND COMPETITIVE GAMING 58

CHAPTER 18: BREAKING INTO THE GAMING INDUSTRY 61

CHAPTER 19: NETWORKING AND BUILDING CONNECTIONS 64

CHAPTER 20: NAVIGATING JOB INTERVIEWS IN THE VIDEO GAME INDUSTRY 68

CHAPTER 21: RESUMES AND COVER LETTERS FOR GAME PROFESSIONALS 71

CHAPTER 22: NEGOTIATING SALARIES AND CONTRACTS 74

CHAPTER 23: BALANCING WORK AND PERSONAL LIFE 77

CHAPTER 24: FREELANCING IN THE VIDEO GAME INDUSTRY 80

CHAPTER 25: STARTING YOUR INDEPENDENT GAME STUDIO 84

CHAPTER 26: CHALLENGES AND OPPORTUNITIES IN MOBILE GAMING   87

CHAPTER 27: THE WORLD OF AUGMENTED REALITY GAMES   90

CHAPTER 28: VIRTUAL REALITY GAMING AND POSSIBILITIES   94

CHAPTER 29: ETHICAL CONSIDERATIONS IN VIDEO GAME DEVELOPMENT   97

CHAPTER 30: GAME LOCALIZATION AND INTERNATIONAL MARKETS   100

CHAPTER 33: DEALING WITH ONLINE HARASSMENT AND TOXICITY   109

CHAPTER 34: GAMING FOR SOCIAL IMPACT   112

CHAPTER 35: GAMIFICATION IN EDUCATION AND TRAINING   116

CHAPTER 36: EXPLORING ALTERNATIVE CAREER PATHS IN GAMING   119

CHAPTER 37: CONTINUING EDUCATION AND PROFESSIONAL DEVELOPMENT   123

CHAPTER 38: STAYING COMPETITIVE IN THE FAST-PACED GAMING INDUSTRY   128

CHAPTER 39: THE FUTURE OF VIDEO GAME INDUSTRY 131

CHAPTER 40: YOUR JOURNEY BEGINS HERE 134

Introduction

Welcome to *Ctrl+Alt+Achieve: A Roadmap for Young Adults Pursuing the Video Game Industry*! This book is designed to be your comprehensive guide as you embark on your journey into the exciting world of the video game industry. Whether you dream of becoming a game designer, a programmer, a sound designer, or any other role within the industry, this book will provide you with the knowledge, guidance, and resources you need to succeed. The video game industry is a rapidly growing field that offers a wide range of career opportunities. With advancements in technology and the ever-increasing popularity of gaming, now is the perfect time to dive into this dynamic industry. However, the path to success in the gaming industry can be challenging and competitive. That is why this book is here to help you navigate through the complexities and make the most out of your journey. In this book, we will explore various aspects of the video game industry, from the basics of game design to the intricacies of marketing and distribution. Each chapter will delve into a specific topic, providing you with practical advice, industry insights, and real-world examples. Whether you are a beginner just starting out or someone already familiar with the industry, there will be valuable information for everyone in this book. Throughout this book, you will learn how to build your video game portfolio, master game design principles, acquire programming fundamentals, and explore different game development engines. You will also discover how to create your first Roblox game, increase user engagement, and monetize your creations.
Furthermore, we will delve into important topics such as user experience design, 3D graphics, sound design, game testing, marketing strategies, and much more. In addition, this book will provide guidance on breaking into the

gaming industry, building connections, and navigating job interviews. We will also explore alternative career paths, such as freelancing and starting your own independent game studio. Furthermore, we will discuss the ethical considerations in game development, diversity and inclusion in the industry, and the impact of gaming on society. As you progress through this book, you will gain a deeper understanding of the video game industry and the skills needed to thrive within it. We encourage you to actively engage with the content, take notes, and apply the knowledge to your own journey. Remember, success in the gaming industry requires passion, dedication, and continuous learning. So, are you ready to embark on this exciting adventure? Let's begin our journey together and Ctrl+Alt+Achieve in the world of video games!Understanding the Video Game Industry The video game industry has experienced remarkable growth and evolution over the past few decades. It is no longer just a niche hobby but a multi-billion dollar industry that rivals the film and music industries. This chapter aims to provide you with a comprehensive understanding of the video game industry, its history, key players, and various sectors within it. 1.1 History of Video Games 1.2 The Current State of the Video Game Industry 1.3 Key Players in the Video Game Industry 1.4 The Different Sectors within the Video Game Industry 1.4.1 Game Development 1.4.2 Game Design 1.4.3 Game Art and Animation 1.4.4 Game Programming 1.4.5 Game Testing and Quality Assurance 1.4.6 Game Sound Design 1.4.7 Game Marketing and Publishing 1.4.8 Esports and Competitive Gaming 1.4.9 Mobile Gaming 1.5 Trends and Innovations in the Video Game Industry 1.5.1 Virtual Reality (VR) and Augmented Reality (AR) 1.5.2 Cloud Gaming 1.5.3 Game Streaming 1.5.4 Indie Game Development 1.5.5 Free-to-play and Microtransactions Understanding the history of video games is crucial to gaining insights into the industry's evolution and where it stands today. From the humble beginnings of arcade games and home consoles to modern mobile gaming and virtual reality, the industry has come a long way. We will explore the key milestones and significant technological advancements that have shaped the industry as we know it. Next, we will delve into the current state of the video game industry, highlighting its staggering growth and global reach. We will discuss the economic impact of the industry, including the revenue generated by game sales, subscriptions, and in-game purchases. By understanding the market size and potential, you can gauge the opportunities available to aspiring video game professionals. In any industry, it is important to know the key players and their contributions. We will explore the major companies and developers that have made significant contributions to the video game industry and revolutionized the way games are created, marketed, and consumed. This knowledge will help you stay informed about the industry's leaders and understand their impact on the market. To provide a comprehensive overview, we will explore the different sectors within the video game industry. From game development to marketing and publishing, each sector plays a crucial role in bringing a game to life and ensuring its success. Understanding these sectors will provide you with a well-rounded perspective of the industry and help you identify potential career paths. Furthermore, we will discuss emerging trends and innovations that are shaping the future of the video game industry. Technologies like virtual reality, augmented reality, cloud gaming, and indie game development have opened up new possibilities and expanded the horizons of game design and player experiences. By staying up to date with these trends, you can position yourself as a forward-thinking professional in the industry. Understanding the video game industry is a crucial first step for anyone aspiring to pursue a career in this dynamic field. By gaining knowledge about its history, key players, sectors, and trends, you will be well-equipped to navigate the exciting and ever-evolving world of video games. So, let's dive into the fascinating world of video game industry and discover the endless possibilities it holds.

Chapter 2: The Path to Becoming a Video Game Professional

In this chapter, we will explore the different paths you can take to become a video game professional. Whether you dream of being a game designer, programmer, artist, or sound designer, there are various routes you can pursue to achieve your goals.

1. Discover Your Passion

The first step on your journey to becoming a video game professional is to discover your passion within the industry. Take the time to introspect and identify the specific role or area that excites you the most. Are you interested in creating immersive virtual worlds as a game designer? Or do you have a knack for coding and want to become a game programmer? Finding your passion will give you direction and motivation as you embark on this career path.

2. Gain relevant education

While a formal education is not always a requirement in the video game industry, it can greatly enhance your skills and make you stand out to potential employers. Consider pursuing a degree in game design, computer science, or a related field. These programs often provide a strong foundation in the technical and creative aspects of game development. Additionally, there are many online courses, tutorials, and workshops available that can help you develop specific skills needed in the video game industry. Take advantage of these resources to continuously learn and improve your craft.

3. Build a portfolio

One of the most important elements in the video game industry is having a well-rounded portfolio that showcases your skills and creativity. As you learn and develop your skills, work on personal game projects or collaborate with others on small-scale games. This will not only give you valuable experience but will also provide tangible examples of your work to show potential employers. Include a variety of projects in your portfolio that highlight different aspects of game development, such as game design documents, code snippets, artwork, animations, and sound design samples. This will demonstrate your versatility and adaptability within the industry.

4. Seek internships and entry-level positions

To gain practical experience and make connections within the industry, consider applying for internships or entry-level positions at game studios or companies. These opportunities can provide valuable hands-on experience and allow you to learn from seasoned professionals in the field. Even if the position is not in your desired role, any experience within the industry can be beneficial in the long run. It will give you a chance to understand the dynamics of game development, work in a team environment, and build a network of industry contacts.

5. Attend industry events and conferences

To further immerse yourself in the video game industry and stay up-to-date with the latest trends and technologies, make it a priority to attend industry events and conferences. These events often offer opportunities to connect with professionals, attend workshops and presentations, and showcase your portfolio. Networking at these events can be invaluable in establishing relationships with industry insiders and potentially opening doors for future opportunities. Keep an eye out for game jams, hackathons, and other game-related events happening in your local area as well.

6. Continuously learn and adapt

The video game industry is constantly evolving, with new technologies and trends emerging all the time. It is crucial to stay up-to-date with the latest developments and continuously learn new skills. Set aside time for self-improvement and explore emerging technologies and platforms, such as virtual reality, augmented reality, and mobile gaming. Participate in online communities, forums, and discussion boards where you can learn from and connect with other game professionals. Always be open to feedback and critique, as it is through continuous learning and adaptation that you will grow as a video game professional. By following these steps and staying committed to your passion, you can pave the way towards a successful career in the vibrant and ever-expanding video game industry. Stay tuned for the next chapter which will focus on building your video game portfolio!

Chapter 3: Building Your Video Game Portfolio

In the competitive world of the video game industry, having a strong portfolio can make all the difference when applying for jobs or showcasing your skills to potential clients. A portfolio is a collection of your best work that demonstrates your expertise, creativity, and problem-solving abilities.

Why is a Video Game Portfolio Important?

A video game portfolio serves as a visual representation of your capabilities and accomplishments. It allows you to showcase your proficiency in specific areas of game development, such as game design, programming, level design, or art. A well-curated portfolio can impress employers and help you stand out from other candidates. Building a video game portfolio is not only crucial for aspiring game developers but for professionals looking to progress in their careers. It is a continuous process that should evolve as you gain more experience and acquire new skills. Whether you are a student, a hobbyist, or a seasoned professional, the portfolio is your ticket to opening doors in the game industry.

What Should Your Video Game Portfolio Include?

1.

Diverse Projects:

Your portfolio should showcase a variety of projects to highlight your versatility and range of skills. Include different types of games, such as platformers, puzzle games, or role-playing games, to demonstrate your ability to work on various genres. 2.

Quality over Quantity:

It is essential to prioritize quality over quantity when selecting projects for your portfolio. Rather than showcasing every project you have worked on, choose those that best demonstrate your skills and creativity. Select projects that have a clear vision, polished design, and engaging gameplay. 3.

Documentation:

Providing documentation for your projects can give potential employers or clients a deeper understanding of your work process and problem-solving abilities. Include concept art, design documents, code snippets, and any other relevant resources that demonstrate your thought process and attention to detail. 4.

Collaborative Projects:

If you have collaborated with others on game development projects, include them in your portfolio. This showcases your ability to work in a team and collaborate effectively, which is highly valued in the industry. 5.

Showcasing your Skills:

Highlight your expertise by including samples of your work in specific areas, such as programming, art, level design, or sound design. For example, if you excel in programming, include playable prototypes or code snippets that demonstrate your technical abilities. If you are an artist, showcase your best character designs, environments, or animations. 6.

User Feedback and Success Stories:

Including user feedback, testimonials, or success stories from your previous projects can add credibility to your portfolio. It demonstrates that your work has resonated with players and has been positively received. 7.

Online Presence:

In addition to a physical portfolio, it is essential to have an online presence. Create a website or use portfolio platforms like ArtStation, Behance, or GitHub to showcase your work digitally. This allows potential employers or clients to easily access and review your portfolio.

Tips for Building an Effective Video Game Portfolio

1.

Quality Assurance:

Ensure that all the projects in your portfolio are thoroughly tested and free of bugs or glitches. Presenting polished and error-free work demonstrates your attention to detail and dedication to excellence. 2.

Stay Updated:

Keep your portfolio up to date with your latest projects and skills. The game industry is constantly evolving, so it is essential to showcase your ability to adapt and learn new technologies or trends. 3.

Seek Feedback:

Reach out to mentors, professionals, or fellow game developers for feedback on your portfolio. Constructive criticism can help you improve and refine your work. 4.

Continuously Expand and Improve:

Building a strong portfolio is an ongoing process. Even after landing a job or securing clients, continue to work on personal projects and update your portfolio regularly to reflect your growth and progress. Building a video game portfolio requires time, effort, and dedication. It is a reflection of your passion and commitment to the video game industry. Remember, the quality and diversity of your portfolio can significantly impact your chances of success in the competitive world of video game development. Now that you understand the importance of building a video game portfolio, the next chapter will delve into the principles of game design. Stay focused, keep refining your skills, and let your creativity shine through your portfolio -

your gateway to a successful career in the video game industry.

Chapter 4: Mastering Game Design Principles

In this chapter, we will dive into the world of game design principles and explore what it takes to create engaging and immersive gaming experiences. Game design is a critical aspect of the video game industry, as it forms the foundation of any successful game. It combines art, storytelling, and technical skills to create a captivating experience for players.

The Importance of Game Design

Game design is more than just creating pretty graphics or fun gameplay mechanics. It is about crafting an experience that resonates with players and keeps them coming back for more. Good game design can make the difference between a forgettable game and a memorable one.

Game designers are responsible for defining the rules, objectives, and overall structure of a game. They create the gameplay mechanics, balance challenges and rewards, design levels, create characters and narratives, and ensure a seamless user experience.

The Elements of Game Design

There are several key elements that go into designing a successful game:

1. Game Mechanics

Game mechanics refer to the rules and systems that govern how the game works. This includes things like movement, combat, puzzle-solving, resource management, and more. Good game mechanics provide a sense of challenge and mastery, while also being intuitive and easy to understand.

2. Level Design

Level design involves creating the physical spaces and environments in which the game takes place. It includes the layout of the game world, placement of obstacles and rewards, and the overall progression of the game. Well-designed levels are balanced, offer variety, and provide the player with a sense of exploration and discovery.

3. Storytelling and Narrative

Storytelling plays a crucial role in many games, helping to immerse players in the game world and engage them emotionally. Game designers create compelling narratives, interesting characters, and impactful storytelling moments that enhance the player's experience.

4. User Experience (UX)

User experience refers to how players interact with and feel while playing a game. Game designers focus on creating intuitive controls, clear instructions, and smooth gameplay to ensure a positive and enjoyable experience. They also consider factors like accessibility, player feedback, and overall game flow.

Developing Game Design Skills

Mastering game design principles requires a combination of creativity, technical skills, and a deep understanding of player psychology. Here are some tips to help you develop your game design skills:

1. Play and Analyze Games

Playing a wide variety of games from different genres will help you understand what makes a game enjoyable and engaging. Take note of the game mechanics, level design, storytelling elements, and how they contribute to the overall experience.

2. Study Game Design Theory

There are many resources available that delve into game design theory and principles. Books, online courses, and game design communities can provide valuable insights and techniques to enhance your understanding of game design.

3. Practice Game Design

The best way to improve your game design skills is through hands-on practice. Start by designing small games or creating modifications for existing games. Experiment with different mechanics, level designs, and narratives to hone your skills.

4. Seek Feedback and Iterate

Sharing your game designs with others and seeking feedback can help you identify areas for improvement. Take feedback constructively and use it to refine your designs. Iteration is a crucial part of the game design process.

By mastering game design principles, you will be able to create captivating gaming experiences that resonate with players. Remember, game design is an ever-evolving field, so it's important to stay updated with the latest trends and continue learning and experimenting.

Now that you have a good understanding of game design principles, let's move on to Chapter 5: Programming Fundamentals for Video Games.

Chapter 5: Programming Fundamentals for Video Games

Programming is a crucial skill in the video game industry. It is the foundation upon which games are built. Whether you dream of creating your own indie game, working for a big game development studio, or even designing mods or custom content, understanding programming is essential.

The Importance of Programming in Video Games

Programming is what brings a video game to life. It allows you to control characters, create interactive environments, implement gameplay mechanics, and much more. Without programming, a game would simply be a static image or animation. By learning programming fundamentals, you gain the power to create your own unique gaming experiences. You can turn your creative ideas into playable realities. It opens up a world of possibilities where you can shape and mold your virtual worlds.

Getting Started with Programming

If you're new to programming, it can seem daunting at first. However, with dedication and practice, anyone can learn and master programming concepts. Here are some steps to get started:

1. Choose a Programming Language

There are numerous programming languages used in game development, so it's important to choose one to focus on. Some popular choices include: - C++: Widely used in professional game development due to its performance and versatility. - C#: Commonly used in game development engines like Unity and is known for its ease of use. - Python: Beginner-friendly and great for prototyping and scripting in game development.

2. Begin with the Basics

Start by understanding the basic concepts of programming, such as variables, data types, conditional statements, loops, and functions. These concepts serve as the building blocks of any programming language. Online tutorials, video courses, and coding challenges can be great resources to help you grasp these fundamental concepts. Practice writing simple programs to reinforce your understanding.

3. Learn Game-Specific Programming Techniques

Once you have a solid understanding of the basics, dive into game-specific programming techniques. This includes learning about game loops, collision detection, input handling, artificial intelligence, and more. There are plenty of online resources, forums, and libraries dedicated to game development that can guide you in mastering these techniques. Practice implementing these techniques in small projects to enhance your skills.

4. Build Projects

One of the best ways to reinforce your programming skills is by building projects. Start small, and gradually work your way up to more complex games or interactive experiences. You can create simple text-based games, 2D platformers, puzzle games, or even explore the realm of virtual reality. The key is to continuously challenge yourself and build upon what you have learned.

Continuing Education and Growth

The field of programming is constantly evolving, and it's essential to keep up with new technologies and frameworks. Continuously learning through online courses, attending workshops, joining game development communities, and experimenting with new tools will help you stay up to date.

Conclusion

Programming is a fundamental skill for anyone pursuing a career in the video game industry. It unlocks the ability to create unique and engaging gaming experiences. By choosing a programming language, mastering the basics, learning game-specific techniques, and building projects, you can develop your programming skills and open doors to exciting opportunities in the gaming industry. So, roll up your sleeves, grab your keyboard, and start coding your way to becoming a video game developer!

Chapter 6: Exploring Game Development Engines

Game development engines are powerful tools that allow developers to create and build video games with ease. In this chapter, we will explore the world of game development engines, discussing what they are, why they are important, and how to get started with them. Whether you are a beginner or have some experience in game development, this chapter will provide you with valuable insights on finding the right game development engine for your projects.

What is a Game Development Engine?

A game development engine, also known as a game engine, is a software framework that provides developers with a set of tools, libraries, and functionalities to create and develop video games. These engines serve as a foundation for game development, offering essential features such as rendering graphics, handling physics, managing game assets, and implementing game logic. One of the key advantages of using a game development engine is its ability to simplify the game development process. By providing pre-built systems and tools, game engines allow developers to focus more on the creative aspects of game design rather than spending time on low-level programming tasks. This makes game development more accessible and efficient for both experienced and novice developers.

Why Are Game Development Engines Important?

Game development engines play a crucial role in the video game industry. They enable developers to bring their creative visions to life by providing a platform to build, test, and deploy games across different platforms and devices. Here are some reasons why game development engines are important for aspiring game professionals: 1. **Productivity:** Game engines provide an extensive set of tools and features that streamline the development process, reducing the time and effort required to create a game. This allows developers to focus on creating innovative gameplay, stunning visuals, and engaging stories. 2. **Compatibility:** Game engines often support multiple platforms, including desktop, console, and mobile devices. This means that developers can use a single engine to create games that can be deployed on various platforms, reaching a wider audience. 3. **Community and Support:** Game development engines have supportive communities of developers who share their knowledge, provide tutorials, and offer assistance. This creates a network of support where developers can learn from others, collaborate on projects, and seek guidance when facing challenges. 4. **Rapid Prototyping:** Game engines allow developers to quickly prototype and iterate on game ideas. With the help of built-in tools and visual editors, developers can rapidly create and test game mechanics, levels, and assets, enabling them to refine their designs and make informed decisions.

Popular Game Development Engines

There are several game development engines available in the market, each with its own strengths and focus. Here are some of the popular game engines worth exploring: 1. **Unity:** Unity is one of the most widely used game engines, known for its versatility and cross-platform capabilities. It offers a comprehensive set of tools for 2D and 3D game development and has a large user community and extensive asset store. 2. **Unreal Engine:** Unreal Engine, developed by Epic Games, is a powerful game engine used for creating high-quality graphics and immersive experiences. It provides an array of tools for real-time rendering, physics simulation, and visual scripting. 3. **Godot:** Godot is a free and open-source game engine that offers a user-friendly interface and a powerful set of features for 2D and 3D game development. It provides a visual programming system and supports multiple scripting languages. 4. **CryEngine:** CryEngine is known for its stunning visuals and advanced rendering capabilities. It has been used to create visually impressive games and offers a range of tools for creating realistic environments and characters.

Getting Started with Game Development Engines

To get started with game development engines, follow these steps: 1. **Research and Evaluate:** Take time to research and evaluate different game development engines based on your project requirements and goals. Consider factors such as ease of use, learning curve, community support, platform compatibility, and licensing terms. 2. **Learn the Basics:** Once you have chosen a game engine, familiarize yourself with its interface, features, and workflow. Many game engines provide official documentation, tutorials, and sample projects to help you get started. 3. **Start Small:** Begin with small projects to gain hands-on experience and learn the intricacies of the game engine. Experiment with different features and techniques to understand how they can be used to create engaging gameplay experiences. 4. **Join the Community:** Engage with the game development community surrounding your chosen engine. Participate in online forums, attend conferences or meetups, and seek feedback from experienced developers. This will help you expand your knowledge and build valuable connections. 5. **Keep Learning:** Game development engines are constantly evolving, with regular updates and new features. Stay updated with the latest advancements, learn new tools and techniques, and continue to improve your skills through continuous learning and practice. In conclusion, game development engines are essential tools for aspiring game professionals. They provide a streamlined development process, a supportive community, and a platform to bring creative game ideas to life. By choosing the right game engine, learning its features, and engaging with the game development community, you can lay a strong foundation for a successful career in the video game industry.

Next Steps

Now that you have a better understanding of game development engines, it's time to explore and evaluate different engines based on your project requirements. Take the next step in your journey by diving into the official documentation, tutorials, and sample projects provided by the game engine of your choice. Remember to start small, experiment with different features, and seek guidance from the supportive game development community. Happy creating!

Chapter 7: Creating Your First Roblox Game

Roblox is a popular online platform where users can create, play, and share games with others. With millions of active players, it provides a great opportunity for aspiring game developers to showcase their skills and creativity. In this chapter, you will learn the steps to create your first Roblox game and bring your ideas to life.

Getting Started with Roblox Studio

To create games on Roblox, you will need to use a tool called Roblox Studio. Roblox Studio is a powerful development environment that allows you to design, build, and test your games. It provides a wide range of features and tools to help you create the game of your dreams. To get started with Roblox Studio, you will need to download and install it on your computer. Once installed, launch Roblox Studio and create a new place, which will serve as the world for your game. You can choose from a variety of templates or start from scratch.

Designing Your Game World

With Roblox Studio, you have complete control over the design and layout of your game world. You can create buildings, landscapes, obstacles, and other elements using the various tools available. Start by brainstorming the concept and theme of your game. Do you want to create an action-packed adventure, a relaxing simulation, or a challenging puzzle game? Once you have a clear vision, start designing the game world accordingly. Use the terrain tools to sculpt the land, add texture, and create hills, valleys, and rivers. Place different objects and assets like trees, rocks, and buildings to bring life to your world. Experiment with different colors, materials, and lighting effects to set the right mood and atmosphere for your game.

Adding Gameplay Elements

Once you have designed your game world, it's time to add gameplay elements to make your game interactive and engaging. Roblox Studio provides a wide range of scripts and tools to help you create various mechanics and features for your game. Start by adding player controls. Roblox Studio provides a set of pre-built scripts that you can use to implement basic movement, jumping, and interaction mechanics for your game. You can also customize these scripts or create your own from scratch to add unique gameplay elements. Next, think about the objectives and challenges in your game. What do players need to do to win or progress? Create scripts that track player progress, award points, or unlock new levels or features when certain conditions are met. Consider adding enemies, power-ups, or collectibles to make your game more exciting. Use scripting to define their behavior, interactions with the player, and rewards. Experiment with different gameplay mechanics to create a fun and challenging experience for players.

Testing and Iterating

Once you have implemented the core gameplay elements, it's important to test your game and gather feedback. Invite friends or other Roblox players to playtest your game and provide their thoughts and suggestions. Take note of any bugs, balancing issues, or areas for improvement. Iterate on your game based on the feedback received. Fix any bugs or glitches, tweak gameplay mechanics for better balance, and make overall improvements to optimize player experience.

Regular testing and iteration are crucial to creating a high-quality and enjoyable game.

Publishing and Sharing Your Game

Once you are satisfied with your game, it's time to publish and share it with the Roblox community. Roblox provides a simple and straightforward publishing process that allows you to make your game available to millions of players. Before publishing, make sure to create an engaging thumbnail and description for your game. These elements will help attract players and give them an idea of what to expect. Consider creating a trailer or promotional video to showcase the unique features and gameplay of your game. When you're ready, click on the "Publish to Roblox" button in Roblox Studio. Follow the prompts to set the appropriate game permissions, select the appropriate category and tags, and upload any required assets. Once published, your game will be available for anyone to play and enjoy.

Continuing Your Roblox Game Development Journey

Creating your first Roblox game is an exciting milestone, but it's just the beginning of your journey as a game developer. Keep learning, experimenting, and improving your skills. Explore different genres, collaborate with other developers, and stay updated with the latest trends and updates in the Roblox community. Remember, game development is a continuous learning process. Embrace challenges, seek feedback, and never stop honing your craft. With dedication and persistence, you can create amazing games that bring joy and entertainment to players around the world. That concludes Chapter 7: Creating Your First Roblox Game. In the next chapter, we will explore ways to increase user engagement in Roblox games.

Chapter 8: Increasing User Engagement in Roblox Games

In the world of video games, user engagement is key. It is important for game developers to create experiences that captivate players and encourage them to continue playing. In this chapter, we will explore strategies for increasing user engagement specifically in Roblox games.

Understanding User Engagement

User engagement refers to the level of involvement and interaction that players have with a game. Engaged players are more likely to spend more time playing, invite their friends to join, and even spend money on in-game purchases. Therefore, it is crucial for Roblox developers to focus on increasing user engagement to ensure the success and popularity of their games.

Creating a Compelling Game Concept

One of the most effective ways to increase user engagement in Roblox games is by creating a compelling game concept. Your game should have a unique and interesting idea that sets it apart from others. Think about what kind of gameplay mechanics, storylines, or visuals will intrigue and captivate players. When brainstorming game concepts, consider what type of games are currently popular and try to find a unique angle or twist that will make your game stand out. Additionally, make sure to have a clear target audience in mind. Understanding the interests and preferences of your intended players will help you create a game that resonates with them.

Designing Engaging Gameplay

Once you have a compelling game concept, the next step is to design engaging gameplay mechanics. The gameplay should be challenging enough to keep players interested and motivated to continue playing, but not so difficult that it becomes frustrating. Consider incorporating elements like rewarding achievements, unlockable content, and multiplayer features. These additions can create a sense of progression and competition that motivates players to keep coming back. Additionally, think about incorporating social elements such as leaderboards or in-game chat features to encourage interaction and collaboration among players.

Regularly Updating and Adding New Content

To maintain user engagement in Roblox games, it is essential to regularly update and add new content. This not only keeps the game fresh and exciting for existing players but also attracts new players who are looking for something new to explore. Consider introducing new levels, challenges, characters, or cosmetic items on a regular basis. This will give players something to look forward to and encourage them to keep coming back to see what's new. Additionally, listen to player feedback and make improvements or changes based on their suggestions. By involving the player community in the game's development, you can increase their sense of ownership and investment in the game.

Building a Community

Creating a vibrant and active community around your Roblox game is another effective way to increase user engagement. Encourage players to interact with each other through social platforms, in-game events, or forums. By fostering a sense of community, players will feel a stronger connection to the game and be more likely to continue playing and recommend it to others. Consider organizing tournaments, competitions, or special events that bring players together. This not only encourages engagement but also creates a sense of excitement and camaraderie within the community.

Using Analytics and Feedback

Lastly, in order to continuously improve user engagement, it is important to track and analyze player behavior and feedback. Make use of analytic tools provided by Roblox to gather data on player activity, retention rates, and purchasing patterns. This information can help you identify areas for improvement and make data-driven decisions to enhance user engagement. Additionally, actively seek feedback from your player community through surveys, forums, or social media channels. Listening to player suggestions and addressing their concerns will not only show them that their opinions matter but also help you understand their needs and expectations better. By implementing these strategies and paying attention to user engagement, you can build a successful Roblox game that attracts and retains a loyal player base. Remember, user engagement is the key to the long-term success and popularity of your game. Stay creative, adapt to player preferences, and continuously strive to improve the overall gaming experience.

Chapter 9: Monetizing Your Roblox Game

Roblox is not only a platform for creativity and game development, but it also offers opportunities for monetization. In this chapter, we will explore various strategies and techniques for monetizing your Roblox game.

Understanding the Roblox Economy

Before diving into monetization methods, it is essential to understand the Roblox economy. Roblox has its own virtual currency called Robux, which can be earned and purchased. Players can use Robux to buy virtual items, accessories, clothing, game passes, and much more within the Roblox platform. When it comes to monetizing your Roblox game, there are primarily two ways to earn Robux: through in-game purchases and through the Roblox Affiliate Program.

In-Game Purchases

One of the most common ways to monetize your Roblox game is by offering in-game purchases. These can include game passes, cosmetic items, exclusive perks, and other virtual goods that enhance the gameplay experience. Here are some popular in-game purchases you can consider implementing in your game:

Game Passes

Game passes are special items that grant players specific abilities, perks, or access to exclusive content within your game. For example, you could create a game pass that unlocks additional levels, provides additional in-game currency, or grants special abilities to players.

Cosmetic Items

Cosmetic items are virtual accessories or clothing that allow players to customize the appearance of their in-game characters. This can include hats, shirts, pants, accessories, and even pets. Players are often willing to spend Robux on cosmetic items to personalize their gaming experience and stand out from others.

In-Game Currency

In some Roblox games, players can earn in-game currency by completing tasks or achievements. As a game developer, you can offer the option for players to purchase additional in-game currency using Robux. This can help players progress faster or unlock exclusive items and features.

The Roblox Affiliate Program

Another way to monetize your Roblox game is through the Roblox Affiliate Program. This program allows you to earn a percentage of Robux from every purchase made by players who have accessed your game through your referral link. To join the Roblox Affiliate Program, you need to have an active Roblox Premium membership. Once you are a member, you can generate referral links and share them with your audience through various channels, such as social media, online forums, or your own website. When someone clicks on your referral link and makes a purchase, you earn a commission in Robux.

Providing Value to Players

Regardless of the monetization method you choose, it is crucial to provide value to your players. Players are more likely to spend Robux on your game if they see the benefits and enjoyment they will gain from their purchases. Ensure that your in-game purchases enhance the gameplay experience, provide unique features, or add value in some way. Continuously update your game with new content, bug fixes, and improvements to keep players engaged and interested in spending Robux.

Promoting Your Monetized Game

Monetizing your Roblox game is just the first step. To attract players and encourage them to spend Robux on your game, you need to promote it effectively. Here are some strategies to consider:

Social Media Marketing

Utilize social media platforms such as Twitter, Instagram, and YouTube to create awareness and generate interest in your game. Share updates, gameplay videos, tutorials, and behind-the-scenes content to build anticipation and engage with your community.

Game Trailers and Screenshots

Create captivating game trailers and screenshots that showcase the unique features and gameplay of your Roblox game. Use visually appealing imagery, exciting gameplay footage, and compelling titles to catch the attention of potential players.

Collaborations

Collaborate with other Roblox developers or influential Roblox content creators to cross-promote your game. This can help expand your reach and attract new players who are already interested in the Roblox platform.

Advertising within Roblox

Consider investing some Robux in Roblox's advertising platform to promote your game within the platform itself. This can increase the visibility of your game and attract players who are actively exploring new games on Roblox.

Conclusion

Monetizing your Roblox game is an exciting opportunity to not only earn Robux but also sustain and grow your game development journey. By implementing in-game purchases, joining the Roblox Affiliate Program, providing value to players, and promoting your game effectively, you can maximize your chances of success in the Roblox monetization ecosystem.

Chapter 10: Understanding User Experience (UX) Design

User Experience (UX) design plays a crucial role in creating successful and engaging video games. It focuses on enhancing the overall experience of players by ensuring that the game is user-friendly, intuitive, and visually appealing. In this chapter, we will explore the key principles of UX design and how you can apply them to your own game development process.

The Importance of UX Design in Video Games

In the highly competitive world of video games, the overall user experience can make or break a game's success. A game with poor UX design may frustrate players, leading to negative reviews, low player retention, and ultimately, poor sales. On the other hand, a game with a well-designed user experience can captivate players, enhance their immersion, and keep them coming back for more. Good UX design entails a deep understanding of your target audience, their needs, preferences, and expectations. By considering these factors and incorporating them into your game's design, you can create an experience that resonates with players and keeps them engaged and satisfied.

The Principles of UX Design

To create a great user experience, it is essential to follow some key principles of UX design. Let's explore a few of them:

1. Usability:

Usability refers to how easily players can navigate and interact with your game. It involves designing intuitive controls, clear instructions, and a user interface (UI) that is visually appealing and easy to understand. By prioritizing usability, you can reduce frustration and ensure that players can easily enjoy your game.

2. Consistency:

Consistency in UX design helps provide a cohesive and predictable experience for players. This includes maintaining a consistent visual style, layout, and terminology throughout the game. When elements behave as expected and follow a logical pattern, players can focus more on enjoying the game and less on figuring out how to use it.

3. Feedback:

Providing clear and timely feedback is crucial for players to understand the consequences of their actions and to feel a sense of accomplishment. Whether it's through visual cues, sound effects, or other feedback mechanisms, players should always know the result of their inputs and actions. This feedback loop is essential for player engagement and satisfaction.

4. Immersion:

Immersive games offer players a sense of being transported to a different world or reality. UX design can enhance immersion by utilizing sound design, graphics, storytelling, and other elements to create a captivating experience. By immersing players in a different world, you can create a memorable and engaging gameplay experience.

Applying UX Design to Your Game Development Process

To incorporate UX design into your game development process, consider the following steps:

1. User Research:

Start by understanding your target audience. Conduct research to identify their preferences, demographics, and gaming habits. This knowledge will help you design a game that resonates with your intended players.

2. Prototype and Test:

Create prototypes of your game's user interface and mechanics, and test them with actual players. Gather feedback and use it to iterate and improve your design. Testing early and frequently will help you identify any usability issues and make necessary adjustments.

3. Simplify and Streamline:

Keep your game design simple and intuitive. Avoid clutter and unnecessary complexity. Streamline your user interface and remove any elements that may confuse or overwhelm players. Remember, players should be able to understand and enjoy your game without a steep learning curve.

4. Iterate and Refine:

Continuously gather feedback and data from players through analytics and user testing. Use this information to refine and improve your game's UX design. Be open to making changes and adjustments as needed to ensure a seamless and enjoyable experience for your players.

Conclusion

Incorporating user experience (UX) design principles into your game development process is crucial for creating engaging, immersive, and enjoyable gaming experiences. By prioritizing usability, consistency, feedback, and immersion, you can create games that resonate with players and keep them coming back for more. Remember to always consider your target audience and actively seek their feedback to continuously improve your game's user experience.

Chapter 11: Building Immersive Virtual Environments

In the ever-evolving world of video games, creating immersive virtual environments is essential for captivating players and providing them with unforgettable experiences. This chapter will delve into the techniques and principles behind building immersive virtual environments and explore the factors that contribute to their success.

The Importance of Immersion

Immersion is the key to transporting players into a virtual world, making them feel fully engaged and connected to the game experience. When players are immersed, they become deeply involved in the game's narrative, gameplay mechanics, and overall atmosphere. This heightened sense of presence and engagement enhances the overall enjoyment and satisfaction of the gaming experience.

Creating Realistic and Believable Environments

To build immersive virtual environments, it is crucial to create realistic and believable settings that align with the game's theme and storyline. Whether it's a post-apocalyptic wasteland, a fantasy realm, or a futuristic cityscape, attention to detail is paramount. Consider the following factors when designing virtual environments:

Visual Design:

The visual design of a virtual environment sets the tone and establishes the game's aesthetics. It includes elements such as architecture, landscape, lighting, colors, textures, and special effects. Strive for consistency and coherence throughout the game world to maintain immersion.

Audio Design:

Sound is a powerful tool that helps enhance immersion. Carefully crafted audio design, including background music, ambient sounds, and character voices, can bring virtual environments to life and create a more immersive experience for players.

Interactivity:

Allowing players to interact with the virtual environment is crucial for immersion. Implementing interactive elements, such as objects that can be manipulated, doors that can be opened, or puzzles that need to be solved, adds depth and realism to the game world.

Utilizing Technology for Immersion

Advancements in technology have greatly contributed to the immersion factor in video games. Here are some technologies that can be used to create immersive virtual environments:

Virtual Reality (VR):

VR technology enables players to step into a fully immersive virtual world by wearing a VR headset. With realistic visuals, 3D audio, and motion tracking, VR offers an unparalleled level of immersion. Developers can leverage VR platforms, like the Oculus Rift or HTC Vive, to create truly immersive experiences.

Augmented Reality (AR):

AR technology overlays virtual elements onto the real world, blending digital objects with the player's surroundings. AR can add an extra layer of immersion by integrating virtual objects into the player's physical environment. Popular AR platforms, such as Pokemon Go and Microsoft HoloLens, have demonstrated the potential of this technology.

Haptic Feedback:

Haptic feedback technology provides tactile sensations to players, further immersing them in the virtual environment. Devices like haptic gloves or vests can simulate the sense of touch, allowing players to feel the impact of virtual objects or the texture of virtual surfaces.

Designing for Immersion

Designing for immersion requires a holistic approach that encompasses various aspects of game development. Here are some tips to consider when creating immersive virtual environments:

Storytelling:

Develop a compelling narrative that draws players into the game world. An engaging story can enhance immersion by creating a sense of purpose and motivation for players.

Consistency:

Maintain consistency in visual and audio design throughout the virtual environment. Ensure that the elements within the game world align with the overall theme and atmosphere.

Attention to Detail:

Pay attention to the small details that can make a significant difference in immersion. Consider factors such as environmental effects, weather changes, and the behavior of non-player characters to create a dynamic and realistic game world.

User Experience Testing:

Conduct user experience testing to gather feedback from players and refine the immersive qualities of the virtual environment. Actively listen to player feedback and make adjustments accordingly.

Conclusion

Building immersive virtual environments involves careful consideration of visual design, audio design, interactivity, and the effective utilization of technology. By creating realistic and believable settings, developers can transport players into immersive worlds that leave a lasting impact. Remember, immersion is the gateway to unforgettable gaming experiences, and crafting immersive virtual environments is a skill worth mastering in the pursuit of a successful career in the video game industry. Continue reading: [Chapter 12: Implementing 3D Graphics in Video Games]

Chapter 12: Implementing 3D Graphics in Video Games

In recent years, 3D graphics have become a key component of video games, allowing developers to create immersive and visually stunning gaming experiences. From realistic environments to lifelike characters, 3D graphics have revolutionized the way we interact with and perceive video games.

The Importance of 3D Graphics

The implementation of 3D graphics in video games has brought a new level of realism and depth to the gaming industry. It allows game developers to create intricate and detailed worlds that players can explore and interact with. 3D graphics have the power to transport players into virtual worlds, making the gaming experience more immersive and captivating. Not only do 3D graphics enhance the visual appeal of video games, but they also contribute to gameplay mechanics. The use of 3D graphics enables developers to create complex physics systems, realistic character animations, and dynamic environments. These elements add depth and complexity to the gameplay, making it more engaging and enjoyable for players.

Implementing 3D Graphics in Video Games

Implementing 3D graphics in video games requires a combination of artistic skills, technical knowledge, and specialized tools. Here are some key steps to consider when implementing 3D graphics in your video game:

1. Conceptualize and plan your game's visual style:

Before diving into 3D graphics implementation, it is essential to have a clear vision of your game's visual style. Consider the genre, theme, and target audience of your game. Research and gather inspiration from existing games or other visual mediums. This will help you establish a cohesive and appealing visual direction for your game.

2. Learn 3D modeling and animation:

To create 3D objects and characters for your game, you will need to learn 3D modeling and animation. There are various software options available, such as Blender, Maya, and 3ds Max, that offer powerful tools for creating and manipulating 3D assets. Take the time to familiarize yourself with these tools and practice creating various objects and characters.

3. Understand lighting and shading:

Lighting and shading play a crucial role in enhancing the realism and atmosphere of 3D graphics. Learn about different lighting techniques, such as ambient lighting, point lighting, and directional lighting, and experiment with them in your game. Additionally, understand the concepts of shading, including materials, textures, and shaders, to add depth and visual interest to your 3D assets.

4. Optimize your game's performance:

Implementing 3D graphics can be demanding in terms of system resources. To ensure smooth gameplay, it is essential to optimize your game's performance. Consider techniques such as optimizing the polygon count of 3D models, using LOD (level of detail) models, and implementing occlusion culling to reduce unnecessary rendering.

5. Test and iterate:

As with any aspect of game development, testing and iteration are crucial when implementing 3D graphics. Regularly playtest your game to identify any visual glitches, performance issues, or design flaws. Take player feedback into account and make necessary adjustments to improve the visuals and overall gameplay experience.

Conclusion

Implementing 3D graphics in video games has become a fundamental aspect of modern game development. By understanding the importance of 3D graphics and following the key steps outlined in this chapter, you can create visually stunning and captivating gaming experiences. Remember to combine artistic creativity with technical knowledge and always strive for optimization and improvement. With practice and dedication, you can take your game's visuals to new heights and leave players in awe of your 3D graphics prowess.

Chapter 13: Sound Design for Video Games

Sound design is a critical element in creating immersive and engaging video game experiences. It enhances gameplay, sets the tone, and adds emotional depth to the overall player experience. In this chapter, we will explore the importance of sound design for video games and provide tips and techniques for creating captivating audio content.

Why Sound Design Matters

Sound design plays a crucial role in enhancing the player's immersion and creating a truly interactive and compelling gaming experience. Here's why sound design matters in video games: 1. Atmosphere and Mood: Sound effects and background music help establish the atmosphere and mood of the game. Whether it's a suspenseful horror game or an upbeat adventure, the audio elements contribute to the overall ambiance and emotional impact. 2. Feedback and Cues: Sound can provide valuable feedback and cues to the player, reinforcing actions or signaling events. For example, the sound of a door opening or a monster approaching can heighten tension and guide the player's decisions. 3. Character and World-Building: Sound design helps bring characters and game worlds to life. Each character can have unique sound effects that reflect their personality and actions, while environmental sounds can make the game world feel rich and dynamic. 4. Immersion and Realism: Sound design adds depth and realism to the gaming experience. From footsteps on different surfaces to the rustling of leaves in the wind, accurate and high-quality audio can transport players into the virtual world.

Creating Effective Sound Design

Now that we understand the importance of sound design, let's explore some tips and techniques for creating effective audio content for video games: 1. Plan ahead: Like any other aspect of game development, sound design requires careful planning. Consider the desired atmosphere, mood, and emotions you want to evoke in your players early in the development process. This will help guide your decisions when creating sound effects and music. 2. Choose the right tools: Invest in quality audio software and equipment to ensure your sound design is of high standard. Popular digital audio workstations (DAWs) include Adobe Audition, Pro Tools, and Logic Pro. Additionally, consider acquiring a good microphone and audio interface for recording and capturing sound effects. 3. Sound effects: Sound effects play a crucial role in reinforcing the player's actions and providing auditory feedback. Whether it's the sound of a weapon firing, a door opening, or an explosion, make sure your sound effects are clear, distinct, and appropriate for the actions they represent. Experiment with layers and variations to add depth and diversity to your sound effects library. 4. Music: Background music can greatly enhance the overall gaming experience. Consider creating original compositions that fit the game's theme and mood. Alternatively, you can license music from talented composers or use royalty-free music from online platforms. Pay attention to dynamics, tempo, and transitions to ensure a seamless and engaging musical experience. 5. Voice acting: If your game includes dialogue or narrative elements, consider hiring professional voice actors or recording your own voiceovers. Well-performed and well-recorded dialogue can significantly improve the player's immersion and emotional connection to the game. 6. Mixing and mastering: Properly mix and master your audio to ensure a balanced and cohesive sound experience. Adjust the volume levels, panning, and spatial effects to create a sense of depth and space. Pay attention to frequency ranges to avoid audio clashes and enhance clarity. 7. Testing and iteration: Like any other aspect of game development, sound design requires testing and iteration. Playtest your game with a diverse group of players and gather feedback on the audio experience. Make necessary adjustments and refinements to ensure your sound design aligns with the player's expectations and enhances their overall gaming experience.

Conclusion

Sound design is a crucial component of the video game industry. It sets the mood, enhances immersion, and provides important audio feedback to players. By understanding the importance of sound design and implementing effective techniques, you can create captivating and memorable video game experiences. So, let your creativity flow and explore the endless possibilities of sound design in your game projects!

Chapter 14: Game Testing and Quality Assurance

Game testing and quality assurance are crucial steps in the development process of a video game. These processes ensure that the game is free from bugs, glitches, and other technical issues, providing players with a smooth and enjoyable gaming experience. In this chapter, we will explore the importance of game testing, the role of a quality assurance (QA) team, and the methods and techniques used in testing video games.

The Importance of Game Testing

Game testing plays a vital role in the development cycle of a video game. It helps identify and fix technical issues, ensures that the game is stable and runs smoothly, and helps deliver a polished product to the players. Here are some key reasons why game testing is crucial: 1. **Bug Detection:** Game testing helps in identifying and reporting bugs, glitches, and other technical issues. These issues can range from minor annoyances to game-breaking problems that prevent players from progressing. By detecting and fixing these bugs before the game is released, developers can enhance the overall experience for players. 2. **Balancing and Difficulty:** Game testing helps in balancing gameplay and difficulty. Testers can provide valuable feedback on whether certain levels or challenges are too easy or too difficult. This feedback enables developers to make necessary adjustments to ensure a balanced and enjoyable gameplay experience. 3. **Stability and Performance:** Game testing ensures that the game is stable, performs well, and runs smoothly on different hardware configurations. Testers can identify performance issues such as frame rate drops, crashes, and freezes, allowing developers to optimize the game for a better player experience. 4. **User Experience:** Game testing helps developers understand how players will interact with the game. Testers provide feedback on the intuitiveness of controls, the clarity of instructions, and the overall user interface. This feedback helps improve the user experience and ensures that players can easily navigate through the game.

The Role of Quality Assurance (QA) Team

A dedicated quality assurance (QA) team is responsible for conducting game testing and ensuring the overall quality of the game. The QA team works closely with the development team to identify and fix any issues that may arise during the testing phase. Here are some key responsibilities of a QA team: 1. **Test Planning:** The QA team creates a comprehensive test plan, outlining the different features and aspects of the game that need to be tested. This includes gameplay mechanics, graphical assets, audio, user interface, and any specific requirements outlined by the development team. 2. **Test Execution:** The QA team performs various tests, following the test plan, to identify bugs, glitches, and other technical issues. This involves playing through the game multiple times, trying different scenarios, and documenting any issues encountered along the way. 3. **Bug Reporting:** When a bug or issue is discovered, the QA team logs it in a bug tracking system. They provide detailed information about the issue, including steps to reproduce it, the impact on gameplay, and any relevant screenshots or videos. This allows the development team to investigate and address the issue effectively. 4. **Regression Testing:** As updates and changes are made to the game based on bug reports, the QA team performs regression testing to ensure that fixing one issue does not introduce new problems. This iterative process helps maintain the stability and overall quality of the game.

Methods and Techniques in Game Testing

Game testing involves various methods and techniques to ensure a thorough examination of the game. Here are some commonly used methods in game testing: 1. **Functional Testing:** This type of testing ensures that all game features, mechanics, and systems are working as intended. Testers play through the game, following specific test cases, to verify that everything functions correctly. 2. **Compatibility Testing:** Compatibility testing involves testing the game on different hardware configurations, operating systems, and platforms. This helps identify any compatibility issues that may arise and ensures that the game runs smoothly across various devices. 3. **Performance Testing:** Performance testing focuses on evaluating the game's performance, including frame rate, load times, and resource usage. Testers analyze the game's performance under different scenarios and provide feedback on areas that require optimization. 4. **Localization Testing:** If the game is intended for a global audience, localization testing is crucial. Testers ensure that the game's text, audio, and visual elements are correctly translated and culturally appropriate for different regions. 5. **User Acceptance Testing (UAT):** User acceptance testing involves gathering a group of players, outside of the development team, to play the game and provide feedback. This helps validate the game's overall experience and identify any potential issues or improvements. In conclusion, game testing and quality assurance are essential steps in the development process of a video game. By thoroughly testing the game and addressing any issues that arise, developers can deliver a polished and enjoyable gaming experience to their players. The role of a dedicated QA team, along with various testing methods and techniques, ensures that the game meets the highest standards of quality and performance.

Chapter 15: Marketing Strategies for Video Games

Marketing plays a critical role in the success of any video game. Without effective marketing strategies, even the most innovative and well-designed games can go unnoticed. In this chapter, we will explore various marketing strategies that can help you promote your video game and maximize its reach and impact.

The Importance of Marketing in the Gaming Industry

In today's highly competitive gaming industry, marketing is essential to stand out from the crowd. By effectively promoting your game, you can create awareness, generate excitement, and drive player engagement. Marketing helps you reach your target audience, build a loyal fan base, and increase your game's visibility in a crowded marketplace.

Identifying Your Target Audience

Before crafting your marketing strategy, it is crucial to identify your target audience. Understanding who your game is designed for will help you tailor your marketing messages and channel selection accordingly. Consider factors such as age group, interests, gaming preferences, and demographics to create a detailed buyer persona that represents your ideal player.

Creating a Strong Brand Identity

Developing a compelling brand identity is crucial for attracting and retaining players. A strong brand identity encompasses your game's name, logo, visuals, and overall tone. It should resonate with your target audience and differentiate your game from competitors. Focus on creating a unique and memorable brand that reflects the essence and experience of your game.

Building a Game Website and Landing Page

Having a dedicated game website is essential for showcasing your game and providing relevant information to potential players. Your website should feature engaging visuals, gameplay trailers, screenshots, and a description that highlights your game's unique features. Additionally, create a landing page with a call-to-action for interested players to sign up for updates or access exclusive content.

Social Media Marketing

Social media platforms offer a powerful and cost-effective way to connect with your target audience and build a community around your game. Identify which platforms your audience frequents the most, such as Facebook, Instagram, Twitter, or Twitch, and create engaging content that showcases your game's progress, behind-the-scenes insights, and upcoming features. Encourage user-generated content, such as fan art or gameplay videos, to increase engagement and reach.

Content Marketing

Content marketing involves creating valuable and informative content related to your game that attracts and retains players. This can include blog posts, tutorials, developer diaries, podcasts, or YouTube videos. By providing valuable insights, tips, and updates, you can establish yourself as an authority in the gaming industry and drive organic traffic to your game's website.

Influencer Partnerships

Collaborating with influencers who have a significant following in the gaming community can help amplify your game's reach. Identify influencers whose content aligns with your game's genre and target audience, and reach out to them for potential collaborations. Consider offering them exclusive access to your game, early copies for review, or sponsored content opportunities to create buzz and generate interest.

Game Events and Conferences

Attending game events and conferences is a great way to showcase your game, connect with industry professionals, and gather feedback from players. Look for local and international gaming conventions, trade shows, and developer conferences where you can exhibit your game and network with potential players, publishers, and investors.

Public Relations and Press Coverage

Securing press coverage and media attention can significantly boost your game's visibility. Develop a press release announcing key milestones or updates and distribute it to relevant gaming news outlets, bloggers, and influencers. Reach out to journalists and work on building relationships with the media to increase your chances of gaining coverage and reviews.

Ad Campaigns and App Store Optimization

Running targeted advertising campaigns can help you reach a wider audience and drive downloads or purchases for your game. Consider platforms like Google Ads, Facebook Ads, or YouTube Ads to reach your target audience effectively. Additionally, optimize your game's metadata, keywords, and visuals on app stores like Steam or the Apple App Store to improve discoverability.

Tracking and Analyzing Marketing Efforts

It is crucial to track and analyze the effectiveness of your marketing efforts to understand what strategies are working and where improvements can be made. Utilize tools such as Google Analytics, social media insights, or app store analytics to measure key metrics like website traffic, conversion rates, player engagement, and user demographics. This data will help you refine your marketing strategy and make informed decisions moving forward.

Conclusion

Effective marketing strategies are a vital component of success in the video game industry. By identifying your target audience, creating a strong brand identity, utilizing social media and content marketing, partnering with influencers, attending events, securing press coverage, running ad campaigns, and analyzing your marketing efforts, you can increase awareness and drive engagement for your video game. Remember that consistency, creativity, and adaptability are key in navigating the ever-evolving landscape of video game marketing.

Chapter 16: Game Publishing and Distribution

Game publishing and distribution are crucial aspects of the video game industry. Once a game is developed, it needs to be published and made available to players. This chapter will discuss the various steps involved in game publishing and distribution, along with some key strategies for success.

Understanding Game Publishing

Game publishing refers to the process of bringing a game to market and making it available for sale or download. Publishers play a vital role in this process as they provide the necessary resources, expertise, and support to ensure the game's success. They work closely with developers to handle tasks such as marketing, distribution, localization, and quality assurance. Publishers have a wide range of responsibilities, including securing distribution deals, creating marketing campaigns, managing community engagement, coordinating PR efforts, and handling customer support. They also provide financial support to cover development costs and take a share of the game's revenue in return.

The Role of Distributors

Distributors play an important role in getting games into the hands of players. They act as intermediaries between game publishers and retailers, ensuring that physical copies of the game reach store shelves or that digital copies are available on platforms such as Steam, PlayStation Network, Xbox Live, or the App Store. Distributors can also help with marketing and promotion, as they often have established relationships with retailers and can negotiate shelf space or promotional opportunities. They handle logistics, such as manufacturing physical copies, shipping, and managing inventory. Additionally, they contribute to localization efforts by ensuring that games are available in multiple languages and tailored to regional markets.

Choosing the Right Publishing and Distribution Channels

When it comes to publishing and distributing a game, it's important to choose the right channels based on the target audience, genre of the game, and available resources. Here are some popular options to consider:

Traditional Publishers:

Traditional publishers are well-established companies with extensive experience and resources in the gaming industry. They typically work with larger game studios and handle the entire publishing process, including marketing, distribution, and localization. However, securing a publishing deal with a traditional publisher can be challenging for indie developers, as they often prioritize projects with commercial potential.

Indie Publishers:

Indie publishers specialize in working with independent developers and smaller studios. They offer more personalized support and flexibility compared to traditional publishers. Indie publishers often focus on niche markets and genres, allowing developers to maintain creative control over their games while benefiting from the publisher's expertise in marketing and distribution.

Self-Publishing:

Self-publishing has become increasingly popular, thanks to digital distribution platforms such as Steam, Epic Games Store, and Itch.io. Self-publishing allows developers to have full control over the publishing process, from marketing to distribution. This option is well-suited for indie developers who want to retain creative freedom and maximize their revenue. However, self-publishing requires additional efforts in terms of marketing, community building, and customer support.

Key Strategies for Successful Game Publishing and Distribution

To ensure a successful game publishing and distribution experience, consider the following strategies:

Build a Network:

Networking within the gaming industry is crucial for finding the right publishing or distribution partners. Attend industry events, join online communities, and build relationships with professionals in the field. Networking can open doors to potential publishing or distribution opportunities and provide valuable insights into the industry.

Create a Marketing Plan:

Developing a comprehensive marketing plan is essential for promoting your game and building awareness among potential players. Identify your target audience, create compelling marketing materials, leverage social media platforms, collaborate with influencers, and consider running targeted advertising campaigns.

Localize Your Game:

Localization is the process of adapting a game to different languages and cultures. This can greatly expand your potential audience and increase the chances of success in international markets. Work with professional translators and consider cultural nuances in your game's content and marketing materials.

Engage with the Community:

Building a strong community around your game is essential for long-term success. Foster a positive and engaging community by actively communicating with players, listening to their feedback, and providing regular updates and new content. This can create a loyal fan base that will help spread the word about your game.

Continuously Improve and Support Your Game:

Post-launch support is key to maintaining a successful game. Actively listen to player feedback, release updates and patches to address issues, and provide excellent customer support. This demonstrates your commitment to your players and can enhance the game's reputation.

Conclusion

Game publishing and distribution are vital components of the video game industry. Whether through traditional publishers, indie publishers, or self-publishing, developers must carefully consider the best channels for releasing their games. By implementing effective marketing strategies, building a strong network, localizing the game, engaging with the community, and continuously improving and supporting the game, developers can increase their chances of success in the competitive gaming market.

Chapter 17: Esports and Competitive Gaming

Esports, or electronic sports, has risen in popularity over the past decade and has become a global phenomenon. Competitive gaming involves professional players or teams competing against each other in various video games. This chapter explores the world of esports and provides insights into the opportunities and challenges it presents.

The Growth of Esports

Esports has experienced exponential growth, with millions of fans tuning in to watch tournaments and championships. Major esports competitions such as The International for Dota 2, League of Legends World Championship, and the Overwatch League have garnered massive audiences and sponsorships from major companies. Esports events are held in stadiums and arenas, and the prize money for tournaments can reach millions of dollars. The growth of esports can be attributed to several factors. The accessibility of online gaming platforms has allowed players from around the world to compete against each other. Additionally, the rise of streaming platforms like Twitch and YouTube Gaming has made it easier for fans to watch their favorite esports events and players. The mainstream acceptance of video games as a form of entertainment has also played a significant role in the growth of esports.

Opportunities in Esports

Esports presents numerous opportunities for young adults interested in pursuing a career in the video game industry. Becoming a professional esports player is one avenue, but it requires exceptional skills, dedication, and a competitive mindset. Players must invest countless hours practicing, honing their skills, and staying up-to-date with the latest strategies and meta-game. However, there are other career paths within esports that don't involve playing the game professionally. Roles such as coaches, team managers, event organizers, shoutcasters (or casters), analysts, and content creators are essential to the success of esports teams and events. These roles require different skill sets, including game knowledge, communication skills, and the ability to entertain and engage with an audience.

Challenges in Esports

While esports offers exciting opportunities, it also comes with its own set of challenges. The highly competitive nature of the industry means that breaking into the professional scene can be extremely difficult. Players and teams must constantly prove themselves through performances in tournaments and consistently rank among the best to attract sponsors and secure contracts. Another challenge in esports is the risk of burnout. The intense training and demanding schedules can take a toll on players' physical and mental health. It is crucial for players to manage their time effectively, prioritize self-care, and maintain a healthy work-life balance.

Skills and Qualities for Esports

To thrive in the world of esports, several skills and qualities are beneficial. Firstly, a deep understanding of the game you wish to compete in is essential. This includes knowledge of mechanics, strategies, and the ability to adapt to changes in the game's meta. Effective communication and teamwork skills are also crucial, particularly for players competing in team-based games. Collaboration, coordination, and clear communication are vital for success in team tournaments. Lastly, determination, perseverance, and a growth mindset are necessary traits. Esports can be highly challenging and competitive, and setbacks are inevitable. The ability to bounce back, learn from mistakes, and continuously improve is crucial for long-term success.

Conclusion

Esports has transformed video gaming into a legitimate career path, attracting millions of fans and lucrative sponsorships. Whether as a player or in various supporting roles, there are numerous opportunities for young adults in the esports industry. However, it's important to recognize the challenges and commit to continuous improvement to succeed in the highly competitive realm of esports.

Chapter 18: Breaking into the Gaming Industry

Breaking into the gaming industry can be both exciting and challenging. With a rapidly growing market and a high demand for talented individuals, it's crucial to take the right steps to stand out and create opportunities for yourself. This chapter will guide you through the process of breaking into the gaming industry and pursuing a successful career.

1. Discover Your Passion

Passion is the foundation for success in any industry, and the gaming industry is no exception. Take the time to explore different aspects of gaming, such as game design, programming, art, sound design, or marketing, and identify which area sparks your interest the most. This will not only help you choose the right career path but also motivate you to continuously improve and excel in your chosen field.

2. Gain Relevant Education and Skills

While passion is essential, it is equally important to acquire the necessary knowledge and skills to thrive in the gaming industry. Research different educational paths, such as degree programs in game design, computer science, or digital arts, and choose the one that aligns with your career goals. Additionally, consider participating in online courses, attending workshops, and joining gaming communities to enhance your skills and stay updated with industry trends.

3. Build Your Network

Networking plays a crucial role in breaking into the gaming industry. Attend gaming conferences, local meetups, and industry events to meet professionals and like-minded individuals. Join online forums, social media groups, and professional associations dedicated to gaming. Building connections and fostering relationships within the industry can open doors to job opportunities, mentorship, and valuable insights.

4. Create a Stellar Portfolio

A strong portfolio can significantly increase your chances of getting noticed by potential employers in the gaming industry. Showcase your skills, creativity, and passion by including your best work, such as game prototypes, artwork, coding projects, or marketing campaigns. Make sure to tailor your portfolio to the specific job you are applying for and highlight your unique strengths and contributions.

5. Seek Internships and Entry-Level Positions

Internships and entry-level positions can provide valuable hands-on experience and help you establish a foothold in the gaming industry. Look for opportunities at game development studios, publishing companies, or gaming agencies. Even if the position is not your dream job, it can serve as a stepping stone toward your ultimate goal.

6. Be Persistent and Apply Widely

Breaking into the gaming industry can be competitive, so it's essential to be persistent and apply to multiple opportunities. Research job boards, company websites, and industry-specific platforms to find available positions. Tailor your application materials to each job, emphasizing your relevant skills and experiences. Don't be discouraged by rejection; instead, use it as an opportunity to learn and improve.

7. Continuously Learn and Stay Updated

The gaming industry is constantly evolving, so it's crucial to be adaptable and continuously learn new skills and technologies. Stay updated with the latest industry trends, follow influential figures, and participate in game jams or online challenges to sharpen your abilities. By demonstrating a commitment to growth and improvement, you'll position yourself as a valuable asset in the gaming industry.

8. Showcasing Your Unique Value Proposition

Differentiate yourself from other candidates by showcasing your unique value proposition. Highlight your specific talents, experiences, personal projects, or innovative ideas that set you apart. Whether it's your exceptional problem-solving skills, ability to create immersive experiences, or a unique perspective on game design, make sure to communicate your distinct strengths to potential employers.

Conclusion

Breaking into the gaming industry requires a combination of passion, education, networking, and perseverance. By following these guidelines and continuously learning and growing, you can increase your chances of creating a successful career in the ever-evolving and exciting world of gaming. Remember, the journey may have challenges, but with dedication and a strategic approach, you can achieve your goal of working in the gaming industry.

Chapter 19: Networking and Building Connections

Building a strong professional network is crucial for success in the video game industry. Networking allows you to connect with industry professionals, learn from their experiences, and open doors for new opportunities. In this chapter, we will explore the importance of networking and provide strategies for building meaningful connections in the gaming industry.

The Power of Networking

Networking plays a pivotal role in the video game industry. It enables you to:

Opportunity for Collaboration

Networking provides opportunities for collaboration. As you build relationships with other professionals, you may find potential collaborators for your projects. Collaborating with others can enhance your skills, broaden your perspectives, and create unique and innovative gaming experiences.

Career Advancement

Networking is crucial for career advancement in the gaming industry. By connecting with industry professionals, you can gain insights into job openings, industry trends, and upcoming projects. Your network can be a valuable source of information and recommendations when seeking new career opportunities.

Learning and Knowledge Sharing

Networking allows you to learn from industry experts and share your knowledge with others. Attending industry events, conferences, and workshops provides opportunities to engage in meaningful conversations, attend informative sessions, and participate in panel discussions. These interactions can expand your knowledge and help you stay updated with the latest trends and developments in the gaming industry.

Mentorship and Guidance

Networking also opens doors for mentorship and guidance. Connecting with experienced professionals can provide valuable mentorship opportunities where you can receive advice, guidance, and support in your career journey. Mentors can offer insights, share their experiences, and help you navigate the challenges of the gaming industry.

Strategies for Building Connections

Now that we understand the importance of networking, let's explore some strategies for building meaningful connections in the gaming industry:

Attend Industry Events

Industry events, such as gaming conventions, conferences, and meetups, are great opportunities to connect with like-minded professionals. Make an effort to attend these events and actively engage with others. Approach people, initiate conversations, and show genuine interest in their work. Remember to bring business cards and follow up with new contacts after the event.

Join Online Communities

Online communities, forums, and social media groups dedicated to the gaming industry are excellent platforms for networking. Participate in discussions, share your insights, and connect with professionals who share similar interests. Engage with others by offering help, seeking advice, and showcasing your expertise. Building a positive online presence can lead to fruitful connections in the industry.

Build Relationships with Peers

Building relationships with peers is highly beneficial in the gaming industry. Attend local game development meetups, game jams, and competitions to connect with aspiring game developers. Collaborate on projects, exchange feedback, and support each other's growth. Your peers can become future colleagues, mentors, or collaborators.

Utilize LinkedIn

LinkedIn is a powerful platform for professional networking. Create a compelling LinkedIn profile that highlights your skills, experiences, and interests in the gaming industry. Connect with professionals, colleagues, and mentors in the industry. Engage with their posts, join relevant groups, and share valuable content to establish your presence as a knowledgeable and passionate individual in the field.

Informational Interviews

Reach out to professionals in the gaming industry and request informational interviews. These interviews give you the opportunity to learn from someone's experiences, gain insights into their career journey, and seek advice on breaking into the industry. Be respectful of their time, prepare thoughtful questions, and express gratitude for the opportunity.

Contribute to the Community

Contributing to the gaming community can help you build connections and establish yourself as a valuable member. Write guest articles for gaming publications, create tutorials, and share your knowledge through blogs or YouTube channels. By providing value to the community, you will attract the attention of industry professionals and foster meaningful connections.

Conclusion

Networking and building connections are essential for success in the gaming industry. By actively engaging in networking activities, attending industry events, and leveraging online platforms, you can establish relationships with like-minded professionals, gain insights, and open doors for new opportunities. Invest time and effort in networking, and you will reap the rewards throughout your career in the video game industry. Stay tuned for Chapter 20: Navigating Job Interviews in the Video Game Industry.

Chapter 20: Navigating Job Interviews in the Video Game Industry

In the competitive job market of the video game industry, a successful job interview can be the key to landing your dream job. This chapter will guide you through the process of navigating job interviews in the video game industry, providing you with tips and strategies to stand out from the competition and impress potential employers.

The Importance of Preparation

Before diving into the interview process, it is essential to understand the importance of thorough preparation. Researching the company you are interviewing with is crucial. Familiarize yourself with their games, their mission, their recent projects, and industry trends. This knowledge will not only demonstrate your enthusiasm for the company but also enable you to ask insightful questions during the interview.

Showcasing Your Skills and Experience

During the interview, you will have the opportunity to showcase your skills, experience, and passion for video games. Be prepared to discuss your previous projects, highlighting any relevant achievements or challenges you faced. Provide examples of how you approached problem-solving and collaborated with others to create successful game experiences.

Highlighting Transferable Skills

Even if you don't have direct experience in the video game industry, you may possess transferable skills that can be valuable in this field. These skills include leadership, teamwork, problem-solving, and creativity. Be sure to emphasize these skills and relate them to how they will benefit you in a gaming environment.

The Importance of Communication Skills

In addition to technical skills, communication skills are highly valued in the video game industry. During the interview, make sure to demonstrate your ability to clearly articulate your thoughts, listen actively, and collaborate effectively. Effective communication is crucial in a team-based industry like gaming.

Answering Behavioral Questions

During the interview, you may face behavioral questions designed to gauge your problem-solving abilities and how you handle certain situations. These questions often begin with phrases like, "Tell me about a time when..." or "Describe a situation when...". When answering behavioral questions, use the STAR method (Situation, Task, Action, Result) to structure your responses. Provide a concise explanation of the situation, describe the tasks you faced, explain the actions you took, and discuss the results you achieved.

Asking the Right Questions

Toward the end of the interview, the interviewer will likely ask if you have any questions. Use this opportunity to demonstrate your enthusiasm and curiosity about the role and the company. Ask questions about the company culture, teamwork dynamics, opportunities for growth, or anything else that will help you evaluate if the position aligns with your career goals.

Follow-Up after the Interview

After the interview, it is crucial to follow up with a thank-you email or note expressing your gratitude for the opportunity to interview. This gesture not only shows your professionalism but also keeps you in the interviewer's mind. Additionally, if you were asked to provide any additional information or samples of your work during the interview, make sure to send them promptly.

Conclusion

Job interviews in the video game industry can be challenging, but with thorough preparation and the right mindset, you can navigate them successfully. Remember to showcase your skills and experience, highlight transferable skills, communicate effectively, answer behavioral questions using the STAR method, ask insightful questions, and follow up after the interview. By following these tips, you will increase your chances of impressing potential employers and securing the job of your dreams.

Chapter 21: Resumes and Cover Letters for Game Professionals

When it comes to pursuing a career in the video game industry, having a well-crafted resume and cover letter is essential. These documents are your first impression to potential employers, and they play a crucial role in whether or not you're selected for an interview. In this chapter, we will discuss the key elements of a successful resume and cover letter for game professionals.

Resumes for Game Professionals

A resume is a concise document that highlights your education, skills, experiences, and achievements. It should be tailored specifically for the video game industry, showcasing your relevant qualifications and showcasing your passion for gaming. 1. **Format:** Start your resume with your contact information at the top, including your full name, phone number, email address, and LinkedIn profile link. Use a professional font and keep the formatting clean and easy to read. 2. **Summary statement:** Begin your resume with a brief summary statement that highlights your key strengths and experiences related to the gaming industry. This should hook the reader and entice them to continue reading. 3. **Skills:** Create a section that lists your skills relevant to the game industry. This may include programming languages, game design principles, software proficiency, and any other technical or creative skills that are applicable. 4. **Education:** Include your educational background, starting with the most recent degree or certification. Be sure to include any coursework or projects that are relevant to the game industry. 5. **Experience:** Detail your work experience, focusing on positions that are relevant to the video game industry. Highlight your responsibilities, accomplishments, and any notable projects or games you worked on. Include internships, part-time jobs, and freelance work if they demonstrate your skills and dedication. 6. **Projects and portfolio:** Showcase any personal projects or portfolio work that demonstrates your abilities in the game industry. Include links to your portfolio website or GitHub repository if applicable. 7. **Awards and accolades:** If you have received any awards or recognition for your work in the game industry, include them on your resume. This can help to differentiate you from other candidates. 8. **References:** Optionally, you can include references from professors, employers, or colleagues who can speak to your skills and work ethic. Make sure to ask for permission before including their contact information.

Cover Letters for Game Professionals

A cover letter accompanies your resume and provides an opportunity to introduce yourself to potential employers. It allows you to showcase your passion for the gaming industry and explain why you are a good fit for the role and company. 1. **Personalization:** Start your cover letter by addressing it to the hiring manager or company. Avoid using generic salutations like "To Whom It May Concern." Research the company and mention something specific that interests you about their games or company culture. 2. **Introduction:** Begin your cover letter with a compelling introduction that grabs the reader's attention. Explain why you are interested in the position and briefly mention your relevant qualifications. 3. **Relevance:** Highlight the skills, experiences, and achievements from your resume that are most relevant to the position you are applying for. Make a connection between your background and the company's needs. 4. **Show enthusiasm:** Convey your passion for the gaming industry and the specific company. Share why you are excited about their games or the impact you believe their products have on players. 5. **Detail your value:** Use specific examples to demonstrate how your skills and experiences make you an asset to the company. Discuss your contributions to past projects, challenges you've overcome, and outcomes you've achieved. 6. **Closing:** End your cover letter with a strong closing statement that reiterates your interest in the position and invites further discussion. Thank the reader for their consideration and provide your contact information. 7. **Proofread:** Before sending your cover letter, thoroughly proofread it for any errors or typos. It's also a good idea to have someone else review it for clarity and effectiveness. Remember, a resume and cover letter are your marketing tools to showcase your skills and experiences. Tailor each document to the specific position you're applying for, and always highlight your passion and dedication to the gaming industry. Good luck on your job search!

Chapter 22: Negotiating Salaries and Contracts

Negotiating salaries and contracts is a crucial aspect of any professional career, including the video game industry. It is important to advocate for fair compensation and to ensure that the terms and conditions of your employment are favorable. In this chapter, we will discuss important strategies and tips for successfully negotiating salaries and contracts in the gaming industry.

Understanding Your Worth

Before entering into negotiations, it is essential to have a clear understanding of your worth as a video game professional. Research and gather information about the average salary range for your role and level of experience. Consider factors such as your skill set, education, work experience, and industry demand. This knowledge will empower you to negotiate confidently and effectively.

Preparing for Negotiations

To negotiate salaries and contracts successfully, it is crucial to be well-prepared. Here are some key steps to follow: 1. Research the company: Learn about the company's financial situation, recent projects, and market position. This information can help you understand the company's ability to offer a competitive salary or better contract terms. 2. Define your goals: Determine your desired salary range, benefits, and any specific terms you would like to negotiate. Be realistic about your expectations and consider the industry standards. 3. Prioritize your needs: Identify your top priorities and must-have conditions. This will allow you to focus on negotiating the most essential aspects during the discussion. 4. Practice negotiation scenarios: Role-play negotiation scenarios with a friend or mentor to build confidence and improve your negotiation skills. Anticipate potential counteroffers and prepare thoughtful responses.

Negotiating Salaries

When negotiating your salary in the video game industry, keep these tips in mind: 1. Start with a higher number: Begin the negotiation with a slightly higher salary range than your target. This provides room for negotiation and allows the employer to meet you somewhere in the middle. 2. Emphasize your value: Clearly communicate the value you bring to the company. Highlight your skills, achievements, and unique qualifications that make you an asset to the team. 3. Consider non-monetary benefits: While salary is important, also consider non-monetary benefits such as flexible working hours, remote work options, professional development opportunities, or equity in the company. These benefits can add significant value to your overall compensation package. 4. Be flexible: Show a willingness to negotiate and be open to alternative solutions. In some cases, the employer may be unable to meet your exact salary expectations, but may be able to offer additional perks or growth opportunities. 5. Take your time: Avoid rushing through the negotiation process. Take the time to carefully review and consider any offers made by the employer. It is important to make an informed decision that aligns with your career goals and needs.

Contract Negotiations

In addition to negotiating your salary, contract negotiations are another critical aspect of securing a favorable position in the gaming industry. Here are some key points to consider: 1. Review the contract thoroughly: Carefully read through the contract, paying attention to the terms and conditions, such as the length of the contract, any non-compete clauses, intellectual property ownership, compensation structure, and termination clauses. 2. Seek legal advice if necessary: If you are unsure about certain legal terms or conditions in the contract, it is advisable to seek legal counsel. An attorney with expertise in the video game industry can provide guidance and ensure your best interests are protected. 3. Request changes if needed: If you find any clauses or terms in the contract that you are uncomfortable with, discuss these concerns with the employer. Offer alternatives or suggest modifications that align with your needs. 4. Be mindful of confidentiality: During contract negotiations, it is essential to maintain confidentiality. Avoid sharing sensitive information about the negotiation process with others, as it may impact your bargaining power. 5. Be professional and respectful: Maintain a professional and respectful tone throughout the negotiation process. Avoid being confrontational or demanding, as it may create a negative impression.

Final Thoughts

Negotiating salaries and contracts in the video game industry requires a combination of research, preparation, and effective communication. By understanding your worth, being prepared, and following negotiation best practices, you can secure a favorable compensation package and contract terms that align with your career goals. Remember, negotiating is a skill that can be honed with practice, so don't be afraid to advocate for yourself and your worth in the gaming industry.

Chapter 23: Balancing Work and Personal Life

Finding the right balance between work and personal life is essential for both your mental well-being and professional success. In the fast-paced and demanding video game industry, it can be easy to become consumed by work and neglect other areas of your life. However, maintaining a healthy work-life balance is key to long-term sustainability and happiness.

The Importance of Work-Life Balance

Achieving a work-life balance is crucial for several reasons. It allows you to: 1. Avoid Burnout: Working excessively without taking breaks or time for personal activities can lead to burnout. Burnout can have severe consequences on your physical and mental health, as well as your productivity and creativity. 2. Maintain Relationships: Neglecting personal relationships can strain them over time. Building and nurturing a support network of family and friends can provide emotional well-being and support when facing challenges in your professional life. 3. Improve Mental Health: Taking time for yourself and engaging in activities unrelated to work can help reduce stress and improve mental health. Hobbies, physical exercise, and spending time with loved ones are important aspects of self-care. 4. Enhance Productivity: Working excessive hours does not necessarily mean being more productive. Taking breaks and having time for leisure activities can help recharge your energy and increase focus and productivity when you do work.

Strategies for Achieving Work-Life Balance

Achieving a healthy work-life balance requires conscious effort and discipline. Here are some strategies to help you create a better balance:

Set Boundaries

Establish clear boundaries between your work life and personal life. Define specific working hours and commit to not working outside of those hours unless absolutely necessary. Communicate these boundaries to your colleagues and clients to manage their expectations.

Prioritize and Delegate

Identify your priorities both at work and in your personal life. Focus on the most important tasks and delegate tasks that can be handled by others. Learning to delegate effectively will help you free up time for personal activities and reduce your workload.

Schedule Time for Yourself

Block out time for activities that rejuvenate and recharge you. Whether it's exercising, practicing a hobby, spending time with loved ones, or simply relaxing, make sure to prioritize these activities in your schedule.

Practice Time Management

Efficient time management is crucial in maintaining a work-life balance. Use tools like productivity apps or calendars to schedule your tasks, prioritize them, and allocate time for breaks and personal activities. Avoid multitasking and focus on one task at a time to maximize efficiency.

Learn to Say No

It's important to learn to say no when you feel overwhelmed or when a request doesn't align with your priorities. Taking on too many commitments can lead to stress and the neglect of personal time.

Seek Support

Don't hesitate to seek support from colleagues, friends, or family when you need it. Communicate openly about your challenges and ask for help when necessary. Building a support network can provide valuable guidance and encouragement.

Unplug and Disconnect

Make it a habit to disconnect from work-related technology during your personal time. Avoid checking emails or responding to work-related messages outside of your working hours. Give yourself permission to fully disconnect and be present in your personal life.

Striking the Balance

Finding the right balance between work and personal life is an ongoing process. It requires constant evaluation and adjustment based on changing circumstances and priorities. Remember that achieving a balance is not about dividing your time equally between work and personal life. It's about aligning your actions with your values and priorities, so you can lead a fulfilling and rewarding life both personally and professionally. By prioritizing self-care and setting boundaries, you'll be able to maintain a healthy work-life balance that allows you to thrive not only in your career but also in your personal life. Remember, achieving success in the video game industry is important, but so is your overall well-being and happiness.

Chapter 24: Freelancing in the Video Game Industry

Freelancing in the video game industry can be an exciting and rewarding career path. It offers the flexibility to work on a variety of projects, collaborate with different teams, and showcase your skills to potential clients. Whether you are a game designer, programmer, artist, sound designer, or any other video game professional, freelancing can be a great way to gain experience, build your portfolio, and establish your reputation in the industry.

The Benefits of Freelancing

Freelancing in the video game industry comes with several benefits. Here are some reasons why many professionals choose to take the freelance route: 1. Flexibility: As a freelancer, you have the freedom to choose when and where you work. This flexibility allows you to set your own schedule, work on multiple projects simultaneously, and take breaks when needed. It also gives you the opportunity to explore different types of work and expand your skill set. 2. Diverse Projects: Freelancing gives you the chance to work on a variety of projects with different clients. This allows you to gain a broad range of experience and develop expertise in multiple areas of game development. It also exposes you to different game genres, platforms, and technologies, expanding your knowledge and making you a more versatile professional. 3. Independence: Freelancing allows you to be your own boss. You have the autonomy to make decisions, set your rates, and choose the clients and projects that align with your interests and goals. This level of independence can be empowering and provide a sense of fulfillment in your work. 4. Networking Opportunities: Freelancing often involves collaborating with different teams, studios, and clients. This provides valuable networking opportunities that can lead to future collaborations and job opportunities. Building a strong network of industry professionals can open doors to new projects, referrals, and mentorship. 5. Portfolio Development: Freelancing gives you the chance to build an impressive portfolio of work. Each project you undertake adds to your body of work, showcasing your skills and expertise to potential clients and employers. A strong portfolio is essential for establishing credibility and attracting new clients in the competitive video game industry.

Challenges of Freelancing

While freelancing in the video game industry can be rewarding, it also comes with its own set of challenges. It's important to be aware of these challenges and take steps to overcome them: 1. Irregular Income: Freelancing can be unpredictable, and your income may fluctuate from month to month. It's crucial to budget wisely and set aside savings to manage periods of lower income. Additionally, diversifying your client base and securing long-term projects can help stabilize your income as a freelancer. 2. Finding Clients: Finding clients as a freelancer requires proactive marketing and networking efforts. It may take time and effort to build a solid client base and secure consistent work. You will need to invest in self-promotion, pitch your services to potential clients, and demonstrate the value you can bring to their projects. 3. Time Management: Working as a freelancer requires self-discipline and effective time management skills. You are solely responsible for managing your project deadlines, prioritizing tasks, and balancing multiple projects simultaneously. Developing strong organizational skills and employing project management tools can help you stay on track and deliver high-quality work on time. 4. Self-Motivation: As a freelancer, you don't have a supervisor or team members to provide constant guidance and motivation. It's important to stay self-motivated and hold yourself accountable for meeting your goals and deadlines. Setting clear objectives, creating a routine, and maintaining a positive mindset can help you stay focused and productive.

Tips for Success as a Freelancer

To thrive as a freelancer in the video game industry, consider the following tips: 1. Specialize: Identify your niche and develop specialized skills in a specific area of game development. Being a specialist in a particular domain can make you stand out from the competition and attract clients seeking expertise in that area. 2. Build a Strong Portfolio: Continuously update and refine your portfolio to showcase your best work. Include a variety of projects that demonstrate your skills and versatility. Aim to present a cohesive and visually appealing portfolio that highlights your unique strengths. 3. Network: Attend industry events, join online communities, and connect with other professionals in the video game industry. Building relationships and networking can lead to new opportunities, collaborations, and referrals. 4. Market Yourself: Invest in self-promotion by creating a professional website, maintaining an active presence on social media, and showcasing your work on platforms like Behance or ArtStation. Utilize professional networking sites like LinkedIn to connect with potential clients and showcase your skills and experience. 5. Communicate Effectively: Establish clear communication with your clients by outlining project goals, timelines, and deliverables from the start. Regularly update clients on the progress of their projects and be responsive to their feedback and inquiries. Good communication builds trust and long-term client relationships. 6. Continuously Learn and Improve: Stay updated with the latest trends, technologies, and industry developments. Invest time in expanding your skill set, learning new tools, and staying relevant in a fast-evolving industry. Continuous learning and improvement will enhance your value as a freelancer. 7. Provide Excellent Customer Service: Exceed client expectations by delivering high-quality work on time and within budget. Be proactive in addressing client concerns, resolving issues, and providing exceptional service. Satisfied clients are more likely to recommend you and provide repeat business. Freelancing in the video game industry can be a fulfilling and lucrative career path for those with a passion for game development. By leveraging your skills, building a strong network, and continuously improving your craft, you can navigate the challenges and create a successful freelance business in the dynamic world of video games.

Chapter 25: Starting Your Independent Game Studio

Starting your own independent game studio is an exciting and challenging endeavor. It gives you the opportunity to bring your creative vision to life, work on projects you are passionate about, and have full control over your career. However, it also requires careful planning, organization, and a strong business mindset. In this chapter, we will explore the key steps and considerations involved in starting your own independent game studio.

1. Define your vision

Before diving into the process of starting a game studio, it is important to define your vision and goals. Think about the type of games you want to create, the target audience you want to reach, and the unique value you want to bring to the industry. This will help you shape your studio's identity and guide your decision-making process.

2. Create a business plan

Like any other business, it is crucial to create a solid business plan for your game studio. This plan should outline your studio's mission, vision, target audience, marketing strategies, financial projections, and growth plans. It will serve as a roadmap to guide your studio's growth and secure potential funding.

3. Build a team

Assembling a talented and dedicated team is essential for the success of your game studio. Determine the roles and skills you need to bring your game ideas to life and start recruiting talented individuals who share your vision. Look for team members with diverse skill sets, a strong work ethic, and a passion for creating games.

4. Secure funding

Starting a game studio requires financial investment. Consider different funding options such as self-funding, seeking investors, applying for grants, or crowdfunding. Develop a detailed budget and financial plan to understand your studio's funding needs and explore all possible opportunities.

5. Choose the right tools and technology

Selecting the right tools and technology is crucial for the success and efficiency of your game studio. Research different game development engines, software, and hardware platforms that align with your game development goals. Take into consideration factors such as ease of use, scalability, and compatibility with your team's skills.

6. Create a development pipeline

Developing a structured and efficient development pipeline is essential for managing your game projects. Define clear workflows, set milestones, and create a project management system that keeps your team organized and ensures efficient collaboration. Regularly review and refine your development pipeline as you learn and grow as a studio.

7. Protect your intellectual property

Intellectual property (IP) protection is important for safeguarding your game ideas and assets. Consult with legal professionals to understand copyright laws, trademarks, and licensing agreements. Take the necessary steps to protect your IP and avoid potential legal issues down the line.

8. Establish a marketing and distribution strategy

Creating a great game is just the first step. Developing a strong marketing and distribution strategy is crucial for getting your game in front of players. Research different marketing channels, build a strong online presence, and develop relationships with influencers and press outlets. Explore different distribution platforms and choose the ones that align with your game's target audience.

9. Continuously learn and adapt

The game industry is ever-evolving, and staying up to date with the latest trends and technologies is essential. Encourage a culture of continuous learning within your studio and invest in the professional development of your team. Adapt to market changes, player feedback, and emerging opportunities to keep your studio competitive. Starting your own independent game studio is a challenging but rewarding journey. By carefully planning, assembling a talented team, securing funding, and establishing a strong business and creative vision, you can set yourself up for success in the dynamic and exciting world of independent game development. Good luck on your entrepreneurial adventure!

Chapter 26: Challenges and Opportunities in Mobile Gaming

Mobile gaming has rapidly grown in popularity over the years, becoming a dominant force in the video game industry. With the advancements in technology and the widespread availability of smartphones and tablets, more and more people are turning to mobile devices as their primary gaming platform. However, with this rise in popularity, there are also unique challenges and opportunities that arise in the world of mobile gaming.

The Challenges

Device Fragmentation: One of the key challenges in mobile gaming is the wide range of devices with varying specifications and operating systems. Unlike other platforms like consoles or PCs, where developers have to optimize their games for a limited number of hardware configurations, mobile developers need to ensure that their games are compatible with a wide range of devices. This can lead to compatibility issues and performance inconsistencies, making it more challenging to provide a seamless gaming experience across all devices.

Monetization: While mobile gaming presents a massive market opportunity, monetization can be a complex task.

There is a higher expectation for free or low-cost games on mobile devices, which puts pressure on developers to find sustainable revenue models. Common monetization strategies include in-app purchases, ads, and premium game downloads. However, striking a balance between generating revenue and providing an enjoyable gaming experience can be difficult. **Discoverability:** With millions of games available in app stores, getting noticed can be a significant hurdle for mobile game developers. Standing out among the competition and getting your game discovered by players can be a daunting task. App store optimization (ASO), social media marketing, influencer partnerships, and user reviews all play a crucial role in increasing the visibility of your game. **Player Engagement:** Mobile gaming typically involves shorter play sessions compared to other platforms. Capturing and retaining players' attention in the limited time they spend playing mobile games can be a challenge. Mobile game developers must focus on creating engaging gameplay mechanics, rewarding progression systems, and compelling content updates to keep players coming back for more.

The Opportunities

Massive Market Reach: The mobile gaming market offers an unparalleled opportunity for developers to reach a massive audience. With millions of active smartphone users worldwide, mobile games have the potential to reach players of all ages and demographics. This access to a vast market allows developers to create games with broad appeal or target niches based on player preferences. **Constant Innovation:** Mobile devices continue to evolve with new technologies, such as augmented reality (AR), virtual reality (VR), and advanced hardware capabilities. This constant innovation opens up exciting possibilities for mobile game developers to create immersive and innovative gaming experiences. Embracing these new technologies can set your game apart and attract players looking for unique and cutting-edge experiences. **Social and Multiplayer Experiences:** Mobile gaming provides a platform for social and multiplayer experiences, allowing players to connect, compete, and cooperate with friends and other players around the world. With the rise of mobile esports and multiplayer-focused games, developers can tap into the social nature of mobile gaming to create engaging and competitive experiences. **Flexible Development Frameworks:** Mobile game development frameworks and engines have become increasingly sophisticated, allowing developers to create high-quality games more efficiently. These frameworks often provide tools for cross-platform development, making it easier to port games to multiple platforms, including smartphones, tablets, and even PCs and consoles. This flexibility allows developers to maximize their game's reach and potentially increase revenue streams. Overall, mobile gaming offers both challenges and opportunities for aspiring game developers. Adapting to the unique demands of the mobile platform, including device fragmentation, monetization strategies, discoverability, and player engagement, is crucial for success. Navigating these challenges and capitalizing on the opportunities can lead to creative, engaging, and financially rewarding experiences for both developers and players alike.

Next Steps

Ready to tackle the challenges and seize the opportunities in mobile gaming? The next chapter delves into the world of augmented reality games, exploring the possibilities of blending the real and virtual worlds to create exciting gaming experiences. So, let's dive in and discover the future of mobile gaming!

Chapter 27: The World of Augmented Reality Games

Augmented Reality (AR) is a technology that blends the real world with virtual elements, enhancing our perception and interaction with the environment. In recent years, AR has gained significant popularity, especially in the world of video games. Augmented Reality games provide an immersive and interactive experience by overlaying digital content onto the real world.

Understanding Augmented Reality

To fully grasp the concept of augmented reality games, it's essential to understand how AR works. Augmented Reality relies on computer vision, cameras, sensors, and GPS to superimpose virtual objects onto the real world. These virtual objects can be seen through a smartphone, tablet, or specialized AR devices like the Microsoft HoloLens or the Magic Leap One. AR games use the camera of the device to capture the real-world surroundings and map digital objects onto them. Players can then interact with these virtual objects and experience them as if they were part of their real environment. This technology opens up a world of possibilities for game developers to create engaging and innovative experiences.

The Impact of Augmented Reality Games

The rise of augmented reality games, most notably Pokémon Go, has had a profound impact on the gaming industry. AR games have the unique ability to blur the boundaries between the physical and digital worlds, creating a more immersive and interactive gaming experience. One of the significant advantages of AR games is that they encourage physical movement and exploration. In Pokémon Go, players have to physically walk around their neighborhoods to find and capture virtual creatures. This aspect of AR games promotes exercise, social interaction, and exploration of new places. AR games also provide a unique social experience. Players can team up and collaborate with others in real-time, creating a sense of community and camaraderie. In certain AR games, players can even see each other's virtual avatars overlaid onto the real-world environment, further enhancing social interaction.

Designing an AR Game

Designing an augmented reality game requires careful consideration of the real-world environment and how the game elements will interact with it. Here are some key factors to consider when designing an AR game:

1. Real-world Integration:

Consider how the virtual objects will interact with the physical environment. Will they blend seamlessly or stand out? Create a design that integrates virtual elements into the real world in a way that feels natural and enhances the overall gameplay experience.

2. User Interaction:

AR games rely heavily on user interaction. Design intuitive and immersive interactions that allow players to interact with virtual objects using gestures, touch, or other input methods. Consider how players will move around and interact with the environment, and design the game mechanics accordingly.

3. Spatial Mapping and Tracking:

Spatial mapping and tracking technologies are crucial for the accurate placement and detection of virtual objects in the real world. Utilize the capabilities of these technologies to ensure that the virtual objects align correctly with the physical surroundings.

4. Performance Optimization:

AR games can be computationally intensive, requiring powerful hardware and software optimization. Ensure that your game runs smoothly on a range of devices, and optimize it to minimize battery drain and improve performance.

Examples of Augmented Reality Games

Pokémon Go is perhaps the most famous example of an augmented reality game. It revolutionized the gaming industry by bringing the beloved Pokémon franchise into the real world. Players could explore their surroundings, catch Pokémon, and battle in virtual gyms. The game's success demonstrated the immense potential of AR games and paved the way for future developments in the field. Other notable augmented reality games include: - "Harry Potter: Wizards Unite," which allows players to explore the

Wizarding World, cast spells, and battle magical creatures. - "Minecraft Earth," a sandbox game that lets players build and explore virtual structures in the real world. - "Ingress," an AR game where players join one of two factions to capture real-world landmarks and gain control over them. These examples showcase the variety of AR games available and the creative ways in which developers can leverage this technology to create unique and immersive gaming experiences.

The Future of Augmented Reality Games

Augmented reality games have already made a significant impact on the gaming industry. As the technology continues to evolve and become more accessible, we can expect even more innovative and exciting AR games in the future. With the advancement of AR glasses and wearable devices, augmented reality games will become even more immersive and seamless. Players will be able to interact with virtual objects and characters in a truly hands-free and natural way. Additionally, as AR technology becomes more integrated with other emerging technologies such as artificial intelligence and cloud computing, the possibilities for AR games will expand even further. In conclusion, augmented reality games have transformed the gaming industry by bringing virtual elements into the real world. These games offer a unique and immersive experience that blends reality and fantasy. With advancements in technology and increasing popularity, the future of augmented reality games is promising, and we can't wait to see what exciting experiences lie ahead for gamers around the world. Keep exploring and discovering new worlds with augmented reality games, for this is just the beginning of a revolution in gaming!

Chapter 28: Virtual Reality Gaming and Possibilities

Virtual Reality (VR) is a rapidly growing technology that has created a new frontier in the gaming industry. With VR, players can immerse themselves in virtual worlds, making it an exciting and unique gaming experience. This chapter explores virtual reality gaming and the possibilities it brings.

The Rise of Virtual Reality Gaming

Virtual reality gaming has gained popularity in recent years due to advancements in technology. VR headsets, such as the Oculus Rift, HTC Vive, and PlayStation VR, have become more accessible and affordable, allowing gamers to experience the virtual world from the comfort of their homes. One of the major attractions of virtual reality gaming is its ability to create a sense of presence. By placing players in a fully immersive environment, VR technology tricks the brain into believing it is in a different reality. This level of immersion enhances the gaming experience and creates a greater sense of presence and engagement.

Enhancing Gameplay with Virtual Reality

Virtual reality has the potential to revolutionize gameplay by providing new possibilities for interaction and immersion. Here are some ways that VR enhances gameplay:

1. Immersive Environments:

Virtual reality allows players to explore and interact with virtual worlds in ways never before possible. Whether it's exploring a fantasy world, solving mysteries in a crime scene, or participating in extreme sports, VR provides an unparalleled level of immersion and engagement.

2. Intuitive Controls:

Traditional gaming controllers and keyboards can sometimes create a barrier between players and the game. With virtual reality, players can use their own movements and gestures to control the game. This natural and intuitive control system adds a new level of realism to gameplay.

3. Realistic Graphics and Sound:

VR technology has made significant advancements in terms of visual and audio fidelity. High-resolution displays and spatial audio systems create a more realistic and immersive gaming experience. Players can feel like they are truly present in the virtual world, thanks to the lifelike graphics and 3D sound.

Potential of Virtual Reality Gaming

Virtual reality gaming has the potential to transform not only the gaming industry but also other sectors. Here are some areas where VR is already making an impact:

1. Education and Training:

Virtual reality has opened up new possibilities for immersive and interactive education and training experiences. From medical simulations to virtual field trips, VR allows learners to engage with the content in a more impactful way. It provides a safe and controlled environment for learning and skill development.

2. Engineering and Architecture:

Virtual reality is being used in engineering and architecture to create virtual prototypes and simulate real-world scenarios. Architects can use VR to walk through their designs, and engineers can evaluate their creations in a more realistic setting. This technology helps in identifying design flaws and improving functionality before the physical construction begins.

3. Healthcare and Therapy:

Virtual reality is being used in healthcare and therapy to treat various conditions. VR provides a distraction for patients during painful procedures, helps in managing anxiety and phobias, and even aids in rehabilitation for stroke survivors and individuals with physical disabilities.

4. Entertainment and Media:

Virtual reality is not limited to gaming. It has also extended its reach into the entertainment and media industries. VR movies, immersive storytelling experiences, and virtual concerts are just a few examples of how VR is transforming the way we consume media and entertainment.

Conclusion

Virtual reality gaming has opened up a world of possibilities for both game developers and players. With its ability to create immersive environments and enhance gameplay, VR has the potential to revolutionize the gaming industry. Moreover, it has applications beyond gaming, including education, engineering, healthcare, and entertainment. As technology continues to advance, virtual reality is likely to play an increasingly important role in our lives, offering experiences that were once only possible in our imaginations.

Chapter 29: Ethical Considerations in Video Game Development

The video game industry is constantly evolving and expanding, with new games being developed and released at a rapid pace. As game developers, it is important to consider the ethical implications of our creations and the impact they may have on players and society as a whole. In this chapter, we will explore some of the key ethical considerations that should be kept in mind during the video game development process. By being aware of these considerations, we can create games that are not only enjoyable and entertaining but also responsible and respectful.

1. Representation and Diversity

Representation and diversity in video games have become increasingly important topics in recent years. It is crucial to ensure that games represent a diverse range of characters, cultures, backgrounds, and perspectives. Developers should strive to create inclusive experiences that cater to players from all walks of life. This means avoiding stereotypes, promoting positive representations, and actively seeking out diverse talent in the development process.

2. Violence and Mature Content

Violence and mature content are often prevalent in video games, and while they can be integral to certain game experiences, it is important to handle them responsibly. Developers should consider the potential impact of violence and mature content on players, especially younger audiences. It is important to provide clear and age-appropriate content warnings, and give players the ability to customize their experiences by adjusting settings and preferences.

3. Player Well-being

Video games have the power to captivate players and keep them engaged for hours on end. However, it is essential to consider the potential negative effects on player well-being, such as addiction and excessive screen time. Developers should implement features that promote healthy gaming habits, such as built-in breaks, time limits, and reminders to take breaks and engage in physical activity. It is also important to provide resources and support for players who may be experiencing gaming-related issues.

4. Microtransactions and Loot Boxes

Microtransactions and loot boxes have been a source of controversy in the video game industry, with concerns about their potential for exploitation and creating addictive behaviors. Developers should approach the implementation of these features thoughtfully and transparently. It is crucial to provide clear information about the odds of obtaining certain items, and to ensure that microtransactions are not predatory or exploitative.

5. Privacy and Data Protection

In our increasingly digital world, privacy and data protection have become major concerns. Video game developers must handle user data responsibly and comply with relevant regulations. Developers should inform players about the data collected, its purpose, and how it will be used. It is important to obtain proper consent and provide options for users to control their data. Additionally, measures should be taken to secure user data and prevent unauthorized access or breaches.

6. Inclusivity in Accessibility

Access to video games should be inclusive for all individuals, regardless of their physical or cognitive abilities. Developers should consider implementing accessibility features to ensure that everyone can enjoy their games. This may include options for customizable controls, subtitles and closed captions, colorblind modes, adjustable difficulty levels, and other features that cater to a wide range of accessibility needs.

Conclusion

Ethical considerations are an integral part of video game development. By addressing these considerations, we can create games that not only entertain but also respect and positively impact players and society as a whole. It is important for developers to continually educate themselves on ethical practices and actively work towards creating a more inclusive and responsible gaming industry.

Chapter 30: Game Localization and International Markets

Game localization is the process of adapting a video game to different languages and cultural contexts, allowing it to be enjoyed by players from different countries and regions. This chapter will explore the importance of game localization and provide insights into the international markets for video games.

The Importance of Game Localization

In today's globalized world, game localization plays a crucial role in reaching a wider audience and maximizing a game's potential success. Here are some key reasons why game localization is essential: 1. Access to International Markets: By localizing your game, you can tap into new markets and reach players who might not understand or feel comfortable playing games in a foreign language. This opens up opportunities for increased sales and player engagement. 2. Cultural Sensitivity: Different languages and cultures have unique nuances and sensitivities. Through localization, you can ensure that your game respects local customs, traditions, and values, thus avoiding unintended offense or misunderstandings. 3. Enhanced Player Experience: When players can understand the game's story, dialogue, and instructions in their native language, it significantly improves their overall gaming experience. Localization allows players to fully immerse themselves in the game world and engage with its content. 4. Competitive Advantage: In a highly competitive gaming industry, localization gives your game a competitive edge. By catering to diverse markets, you can differentiate your game from competitors and attract a larger player base. 5. Increased Revenue Potential: Game localization has a proven track record of boosting sales. Studies have shown that localizing a game can increase its revenue by up to 30%. By expanding your game's reach to new markets, you have the potential to significantly increase your financial returns.

Understanding International Markets

When localizing a game, it is essential to have a solid understanding of the international markets you are targeting. Here are some factors to consider: 1. Language: Identify the languages spoken by your target audience and prioritize localization efforts accordingly. English, Chinese, Spanish, Arabic, and Japanese are some of the most widely spoken languages worldwide. 2. Cultural Differences: Different cultures have unique preferences and gaming habits. Research the cultural preferences of your target markets to customize your game's content and design elements accordingly. For example, certain themes or symbols may have different connotations in different cultures. 3. Localization Quality: Ensure that the quality of your game's localization is top-notch. Hiring professional translators, cultural consultants, and native speakers can help maintain the integrity of your game's content and ensure a seamless player experience. 4. Market

Regulations: Familiarize yourself with the local laws and regulations governing the gaming industry in each target market. Understand any restrictions or requirements for game distribution, rating systems, or content guidelines. 5. Competition and Trends: Research the gaming landscape in your target markets to understand the competition and identify trends. This knowledge can help you tailor your game's features, marketing strategies, and pricing to align with local market expectations.

Successful Game Localization Strategies

To ensure successful game localization, consider the following strategies: 1. Plan Ahead: Incorporate game localization considerations into your development process from the outset. Design your game with localization in mind, allowing for easy integration of translated content. 2. Collaborate with Professionals: Work with experienced localization agencies or freelance translators who specialize in the gaming industry. Their expertise will ensure accurate translations and cultural adaptations. 3. Test and Iterate: Conduct thorough testing of the localized versions of your game to identify any linguistic or cultural issues. Collect feedback from players in the target markets and make necessary adjustments. 4. Maintain Consistency: Create style and terminology guides to maintain consistency across all localized versions of your game. This helps establish a cohesive brand identity and enhances player comprehension. 5. Provide Ongoing Support: After localization, continue to support the international versions of your game through regular updates, bug fixes, and customer service. This ensures a positive player experience and builds customer loyalty. By embracing game localization and understanding the international markets, you can expand the reach and impact of your video game, appealing to a diverse global audience. Keep in mind that localization is an ongoing process, and staying informed about cultural trends and player preferences is essential for long-term success in international markets. Remember, every player's gaming experience should be accessible and enjoyable, regardless of their language or cultural background. Game localization empowers you to connect with players around the world, fostering inclusivity and diversity within the gaming community.

Chapter 31: Diversity and Inclusion in the Gaming Industry

The gaming industry has come a long way in terms of diversity and inclusion, but there is still much work to be done. In recent years, there has been a growing recognition of the need to create a more inclusive and representative industry. This chapter will explore the importance of diversity and inclusion in the gaming industry and discuss strategies for promoting a more diverse and inclusive environment.

The Importance of Diversity and Inclusion

Diversity and inclusion are crucial for the success and growth of the gaming industry. By embracing diversity, game developers can tap into a wider range of perspectives and experiences, resulting in more innovative and creative games. Inclusive environments allow for different voices to be heard and valued, creating a sense of belonging for all individuals. Furthermore, diversity and inclusion are essential for reaching a broader audience. The gaming community is made up of people from various backgrounds, cultures, and identities. By creating games that reflect this diversity, developers can attract a wider range of players and foster a more inclusive gaming community.

Addressing Bias and Stereotypes

One of the key challenges in promoting diversity and inclusion in the gaming industry is addressing bias and stereotypes. Games have often perpetuated stereotypes and excluded certain groups, reinforcing harmful biases. It is important for game developers to be aware of these issues and actively work to challenge and change them. Developers can start by critically examining their own assumptions and biases. This self-reflection can help uncover any unconscious biases that may be influencing game design decisions. It is also important to engage in ongoing education and dialogue about diversity and inclusion in order to better understand the experiences and perspectives of marginalized groups.

Representation in Games

Representation in games is a critical aspect of promoting diversity and inclusion. Players want to see themselves reflected in the games they play, and diverse representation can help foster a sense of inclusion and belonging. Game developers should strive to include characters from different races, ethnicities, genders, sexual orientations, and abilities in their games. However, representation should go beyond surface-level diversity. It is important to create diverse characters that are well-rounded, complex, and free from stereotypes. In addition, diverse representation should extend beyond just the characters themselves and include diverse narratives, settings, and themes.

Creating Inclusive Game Communities

Inclusion extends beyond the games themselves to the communities that surround them. Toxicity and harassment have been pervasive issues in online gaming communities, creating barriers for marginalized groups. Game developers have a responsibility to create safe and inclusive spaces for their players. This can be achieved by implementing and enforcing community guidelines that promote respectful behavior and zero tolerance for harassment. Developing strong community moderation systems and encouraging positive community engagement can also help foster inclusive game communities.

Partnering with Diverse Content Creators and Influencers

Collaborating with diverse content creators and influencers is another way to promote diversity and inclusion in the gaming industry. By supporting and amplifying the voices of underrepresented individuals, developers can help increase visibility and representation in the industry. Game developers can seek out partnerships with diverse content creators and influencers to showcase their games and provide opportunities for collaboration. This can help diversify the perspectives and narratives represented in the gaming community and also expand the reach of their games to new audiences.

Continued Efforts and Progress

Promoting diversity and inclusion in the gaming industry requires continuous effort and a commitment to change. It is important for game developers to regularly assess their own practices and policies, listen to feedback from players and communities, and make adjustments as needed. By actively working to create a more diverse and inclusive industry, game developers can not only improve the quality of their games but also contribute to a more vibrant, welcoming, and representative gaming community. The journey towards diversity and inclusion in the gaming industry is ongoing, but by taking proactive steps and embracing a mindset of openness and inclusivity, we can make meaningful progress. Together, let's create a gaming industry that embraces and celebrates the diversity of its players and creators. Stay tuned for the next chapter: Understanding the Gaming Community.

Chapter 32: Understanding the Gaming Community

The gaming community is a vibrant and diverse group of individuals who share a common interest in video games. Understanding this community is crucial for anyone pursuing a career in the video game industry. By immersing themselves in the community, aspiring game professionals can gain valuable insights, make connections, and learn from others' experiences.

The Power of Community

The gaming community is more than just a group of people who enjoy playing video games. It is a supportive and passionate network that encompasses players, developers, streamers, content creators, and esports enthusiasts. This community plays a vital role in shaping the industry, driving trends, and setting the bar for innovation. One of the most significant aspects of the gaming community is its ability to bring people together. Video games have the power to connect individuals from different backgrounds, cultures, and ages through shared experiences and interests. Whether it's playing multiplayer games with friends, participating in online communities, or attending gaming conventions, the sense of camaraderie within the gaming community is unmatched.

Online Communities and Platforms

The rise of the internet and social media has revolutionized how the gaming community interacts and connects. Online platforms such as forums, Reddit, Discord, and social media groups have become popular gathering places for gamers to discuss their favorite games, share tips and tricks, and form friendships. Participating in online communities is a great way for aspiring game professionals to stay updated with industry news, engage in conversations with fellow gamers, and seek advice from experienced individuals. These platforms also provide opportunities to showcase one's work, whether it's sharing game development progress, promoting a streaming channel, or showcasing fan art.

Streaming and Content Creation

Streaming platforms like Twitch and YouTube have opened up new avenues for gamers to share their gameplay experiences with a broader audience. Many players have turned to streaming as a way to express their love for gaming, entertain viewers, and even build a career as a content creator. Understanding the world of streaming and content creation can be beneficial for aspiring game professionals. By studying successful streamers and content creators, individuals can learn about the qualities that make content engaging and entertaining. They can also gain insights into the preferences and expectations of viewers, which can inform their own game development or marketing strategies.

Esports and Competitive Gaming

Esports has gained significant popularity in recent years, attracting millions of viewers and offering lucrative opportunities for skilled players. Esports tournaments, such as the League of Legends World Championship and The International Dota 2 Championship, draw massive audiences and provide a platform for the best players to showcase their skills. Understanding the esports landscape is crucial for those interested in pursuing a career in competitive gaming or game development. It involves studying popular esports titles, analyzing professional gameplay strategies, and staying updated with industry trends. Building connections within the esports community, such as joining local gaming clubs or participating in online tournaments, can also open doors for aspiring players and professionals.

Cultivating Positive Relationships

In any community, it is essential to cultivate positive relationships and contribute positively. This applies to the gaming community as well. By being respectful, supportive, and inclusive, individuals can build strong connections within the gaming community and create a positive reputation. Engaging with other community members through thoughtful discussions, participating in events, collaborating on projects, or even offering support and advice demonstrates a genuine interest in the community. These relationships can lead to opportunities, mentorship, and collaborations that can further an individual's career in the video game industry.

Conclusion

Understanding the gaming community is paramount for anyone aspiring to succeed in the video game industry. By immersing themselves in the community, aspiring game professionals can gain valuable insights, make connections, and learn from others' experiences. Through online communities, streaming platforms, esports, and cultivating positive relationships, individuals can tap into the power of the gaming community and pave the way for their own success.

Chapter 33: Dealing with Online Harassment and Toxicity

Online harassment and toxicity have become prevalent issues in the gaming community. Unfortunately, the anonymity and distance that the internet provides can lead to individuals feeling empowered to engage in harmful behavior. As a young adult pursuing a career in the video game industry, it is crucial to understand how to navigate and address these challenges. This chapter aims to equip you with strategies to deal with online harassment and toxicity effectively.

Understanding Online Harassment and Toxicity

Online harassment refers to the intentional, repeated, and unwanted behavior directed at an individual or group. It can manifest in various forms, including personal attacks, hate speech, stalking, doxing, and threats. Toxicity, on the other hand, refers to a toxic and hostile environment where individuals engage in negative and disruptive behavior, such as cyberbullying, trolling, and excessive aggression. It is essential to recognize that online harassment and toxicity can have severe emotional and psychological impacts. They can cause stress, anxiety, depression, and even lead to individuals leaving the gaming community altogether. Therefore, it is crucial to address these issues head-on and create a safer and more inclusive gaming environment for everyone.

Implementing Strategies to Handle Online Harassment and Toxicity

1.

Establish Personal Boundaries:

Set clear boundaries for yourself regarding what kind of behavior you are willing to tolerate. This could include muting or blocking individuals who engage in harassment or toxicity. Remember that it is entirely within your rights to protect your mental well-being. 2.

Do Not Engage:

Avoid getting into arguments or retaliating against individuals who engage in harmful behavior. Engaging with them often only fuels the fire and can escalate the situation further. Focus on maintaining your composure and prioritizing your own well-being. 3.

Collect Evidence:

Keep records of any instances of online harassment or toxicity. Take screenshots or save chat logs as evidence to assist you in reporting the individuals involved. This evidence can be helpful if you decide to escalate the situation further. 4.

Report and Block:

Utilize the reporting features available on platforms and games to report instances of harassment or toxicity. Be sure to provide as much detail and evidence as possible when making a report. Additionally, make use of blocking features to prevent further interaction with the individuals involved. 5.

Seek Support:

Reach out to friends, fellow gamers, or community moderators who can provide support and understanding during challenging situations. It is essential to have a support network that can help you navigate through online harassment and toxicity. 6.

Report to Authorities:

In severe cases where there are credible threats or illegal activities involved, consider involving law enforcement. Online harassment can cross legal boundaries, and it is important to take appropriate action to protect yourself and others. 7.

Advocate for Change:

Play an active role in advocating for a safer gaming environment. Support initiatives and organizations dedicated to combating online harassment and toxicity. Encourage community leaders, game developers, and platform providers to implement measures to prevent and address these issues effectively.

Cultivating a Positive Gaming Community

Creating a positive and inclusive gaming community starts with each individual within it. Consider the following strategies to foster a welcoming and supportive environment: 1. Be respectful and mindful of others' feelings and experiences. 2. Speak up against harassment and toxicity when you witness it happening. 3. Encourage positive and constructive discussions within the community. 4. Promote empathy and understanding towards individuals from diverse backgrounds. 5. Support and uplift fellow gamers, especially those who may be facing harassment or toxicity. 6. Educate yourself and others on the harmful effects of online harassment and toxicity. 7. Foster a network of friends and allies who prioritize a positive and inclusive gaming environment. Remember, addressing online harassment and toxicity requires a collective effort from the entire gaming community. By working together, we can create a safer and more enjoyable gaming experience for everyone involved. Next, in Chapter 34, we will explore the impact of gaming for social impact and how video games can be powerful tools for positive change.

Chapter 34: Gaming for Social Impact

Gaming has evolved beyond just entertainment and has become a powerful tool for social change. In this chapter, we will explore the concept of gaming for social impact and how young adults can leverage their skills and passion for video games to make a positive difference in the world.

The Power of Gaming for Social Impact

Video games have a unique ability to engage and captivate players, providing an immersive and interactive experience. This power can be harnessed to address social issues and bring about positive change. Gaming for social impact involves using games as a medium to raise awareness, educate, advocate, and mobilize communities towards important causes. When designed with purpose, video games can not only entertain but also inspire empathy, promote inclusivity, and foster social connections. They can provide opportunities for players to experience different perspectives, challenge stereotypes, and explore complex social issues in a safe and engaging environment.

Examples of Gaming for Social Impact

There are numerous examples of video games that have been created to address social issues and make a positive impact. Let's explore a few notable examples:

1. "Papers, Please"

"Papers, Please" is a game that puts players in the role of an immigration officer in a dystopian world. The game prompts players to make decisions regarding who can enter the country based on a set of complex rules and regulations. It aims to raise awareness about the challenges and ethical dilemmas faced by immigration officers and the impact of immigration policies on individuals and families.

2. "Never Alone"

"Never Alone" is a puzzle platformer game developed in collaboration with Alaska Native storytellers. The game tells the story of a young Iñupiaq girl and her fox companion as they navigate the harsh Arctic environment and face challenges. Through gameplay and storytelling, the game aims to preserve and promote indigenous culture and provide players with insights into the rich heritage of the Iñupiaq people.

3. "Sea Hero Quest"

"Sea Hero Quest" is a mobile game designed to contribute to global dementia research. The game collects data from players as they navigate through various virtual environments, testing their spatial awareness and memory. The anonymous data collected from millions of players helps researchers better understand spatial navigation, which is often one of the first skills to be affected by dementia. This game demonstrates how gaming can be used as a tool for scientific research and contribute towards finding solutions to pressing global challenges.

Creating Games for Social Impact

If you are passionate about addressing social issues through gaming, here are a few steps you can take to make a difference:

1. Choose a Social Cause

Identify a social cause that you are passionate about. It could be climate change, mental health, gender equality, or any other issue that resonates with you. Understanding the key challenges and existing efforts related to the cause will help you create a more impactful game.

2. Design with Intention

When creating a game for social impact, it is important to design it with a clear intention. Define the objectives of the game and how it can raise awareness, educate, or promote action. Consider how the gameplay mechanics, narrative, and visual design can effectively convey the social message you want to communicate.

3. Collaborate with Experts

Collaborate with experts and organizations working in the field related to your chosen cause. Their knowledge and insights will help you create a more accurate and impactful game. Work closely with them to ensure that your game addresses the key issues and presents a realistic depiction of the challenges faced.

4. Engage the Community

Involve the community affected by the social issue in the game development process. Seek their feedback and insights to ensure that the game accurately represents their experiences. This community involvement can enhance the authenticity and effectiveness of the game.

5. Amplify the Impact

Once your game is developed, focus on amplifying its impact. Consider partnering with nonprofit organizations, media outlets, or influencers who align with your cause to promote and distribute the game. Engage with players and collect feedback to continuously improve the game and measure its impact.

Conclusion

Gaming for social impact provides a powerful platform to raise awareness, educate, and inspire action on important social issues. By leveraging their skills and passion for video games, young adults can make a positive difference in the world and contribute towards creating a more inclusive and equitable society. So, let's harness the power of gaming and use it as a force for social change.

Chapter 35: Gamification in Education and Training

Gamification is the application of game design principles and mechanics to non-game contexts, such as education and training. It is a powerful tool that can enhance learning experiences, increase engagement, and improve motivation and retention.

What is Gamification?

Gamification involves incorporating elements commonly found in games, such as points, badges, leaderboards, challenges, and rewards, into educational and training activities. By tapping into the innate human desire for achievement and competition, gamification turns learning into a more enjoyable and immersive experience.

The Benefits of Gamification in Education and Training

There are several benefits to incorporating gamification in education and training: 1. Increased Motivation: Gamification creates a sense of purpose and achievement, motivating learners to actively participate and complete tasks. It provides immediate feedback and rewards, which can boost motivation levels. 2. Enhanced Engagement: Games are inherently engaging and can capture learners' attention more effectively than traditional methods. Through interactive and immersive gameplay, learners are more likely to be actively engaged and invested in the learning process. 3. Active Learning: Gamification promotes active learning by encouraging students to apply concepts and skills in a practical and interactive manner. It allows learners to experiment, make decisions, and learn from their mistakes in a safe and controlled environment. 4. Personalized Learning: Gamification can be tailored to individual learners, allowing for personalized experiences and adaptive learning pathways. By tracking learners' progress and providing targeted feedback, gamification can address their unique needs and interests. 5. Collaboration and Competition: Gamification can foster collaboration and healthy competition among learners. By incorporating social elements, such as multiplayer games or team challenges, learners can work together to solve problems and achieve shared goals. 6. Retention and Transfer of Knowledge: Gamification promotes active engagement and repeated practice, leading to better retention of information and skills. It also encourages learners to apply their knowledge in different contexts, facilitating the transfer of learning to real-life situations.

Examples of Gamification in Education and Training

There are various ways gamification can be implemented in education and training: 1. Badges and Points: Awarding badges and points for completing tasks or achieving specific milestones can provide a sense of accomplishment and progress. 2. Leaderboards and Challenges: Introducing leaderboards and challenges can encourage healthy competition and motivate learners to strive for excellence. 3. Narrative-driven Learning: Creating immersive storylines and narratives can engage learners by giving them a sense of purpose and context for their learning journey. 4. Quests and Missions: Structuring learning activities as quests or missions can make them more engaging and fun. Learners can complete objectives and earn rewards as they progress. 5. Simulations and Virtual Reality: Using simulations and virtual reality technologies can provide realistic and interactive learning experiences. Learners can practice skills in a controlled environment before applying them in real-life situations. 6. Game-Based Learning Platforms: Utilizing game-based learning platforms, such as educational video games or interactive quizzes, can provide engaging and interactive learning experiences.

Considerations for Implementing Gamification

When implementing gamification in education and training, it is important to consider the following: 1. Learning Objectives: Ensure that the gamified elements align with the learning objectives and desired outcomes. Gamification should enhance the learning experience, not distract from it. 2. Feedback and Assessment: Provide timely and constructive feedback to learners to guide their progress. Incorporate assessments that measure both knowledge acquisition and skill application. 3. Balance and Challenge:

Strike a balance between providing achievable challenges and maintaining learner engagement. The difficulty level should be adjusted to suit learners' abilities and promote continuous growth. 4. Inclusivity and Accessibility: Ensure that the gamified elements are accessible to all learners, including those with disabilities or learning differences. Consider diverse learner needs and provide multiple pathways for success. 5. Continuous Improvement: Monitor and evaluate the effectiveness of gamification strategies. Collect feedback from learners and make adjustments based on their experiences and preferences.

Conclusion

Gamification in education and training has the potential to revolutionize the learning experience. By incorporating game design principles and mechanics, learners can engage in active, immersive, and personalized learning experiences. With careful planning and consideration, gamification can effectively enhance motivation, engagement, and retention, ultimately leading to more effective learning outcomes.

Chapter 36: Exploring Alternative Career Paths in Gaming

Many young adults are drawn to the gaming industry because of their passion for playing games. However, pursuing a career in game development or design is not the only way to be involved in the gaming world. There are numerous alternative career paths within the industry that can still be fulfilling and offer exciting opportunities. In this chapter, we will explore some of these alternative career paths and provide guidance on how to pursue them.

1. Game Journalism

One alternative career path in the gaming industry is game journalism. Game journalists have the opportunity to write about and review video games, interview industry professionals, and cover gaming events. They play a crucial role in providing insights and analysis to the gaming community. If you have strong writing skills, a passion for gaming, and a desire to share your opinions and experiences, pursuing a career in game journalism could be a great fit for you. To get started in game journalism, consider creating your own gaming blog or website. Share your thoughts on games, write reviews, and engage with the gaming community. This will help you build a portfolio and showcase your writing abilities. Additionally, reach out to established gaming publications or websites and inquire about any potential freelance opportunities. Building relationships with industry professionals and attending gaming events can also enhance your chances of breaking into game journalism.

2. Game Marketing and Public Relations

Another alternative career path in the gaming industry is game marketing and public relations. Game marketing professionals are responsible for promoting and creating buzz around video game releases. They develop marketing strategies, manage social media accounts, create advertising campaigns, and engage with the gaming community. Public relations professionals, on the other hand, handle the communication between game developers and the media. They organize press events, coordinate interviews, and manage crisis communications. To pursue a career in game marketing or public relations, it is essential to have a strong understanding of the gaming industry and its target audience. Familiarize yourself with marketing and PR principles, and consider pursuing relevant degrees or certifications. Internships or entry-level positions at gaming companies or marketing agencies can provide valuable hands-on experience and help you build connections in the industry.

3. Game Testing and Quality Assurance

Game testing and quality assurance (QA) is another alternative career path within the gaming industry. Game testers play a crucial role in ensuring the quality and functionality of video games. They identify and report bugs, glitches, and other issues during the development process. Game testers need to have a keen attention to detail, patience, and strong communication skills to effectively communicate the issues they encounter. To start a career in game testing and QA, consider pursuing a degree or certification in game development or quality assurance. Familiarize yourself with the various testing methodologies and tools used in the industry. Building a strong portfolio that showcases your ability to identify and report bugs will greatly enhance your chances of securing a job in game testing.

4. Game Localization

Game localization involves translating and adapting video games for different languages and cultures. This is a critical process that allows games to reach international markets and provide an immersive experience for players around the world. Game localizers need to have a strong understanding of different languages, cultural nuances, and gaming terminology. To pursue a career in game localization, it is important to have excellent linguistic skills and a deep understanding of gaming terminology. Consider studying languages and cultures that are in high demand in the gaming industry. Building a portfolio of successfully localized games or working on freelance localization projects can help you showcase your skills to potential employers in the industry.

5. Game Sound Design

Game sound designers are responsible for creating the audio elements that enhance the gaming experience. They design and implement sound effects, music, and voiceovers that bring the game world to life. Game sound designers need to have a strong understanding of audio production techniques, creativity, and a passion for creating immersive soundscapes. To pursue a career in game sound design, consider studying audio production or music production. Familiarize yourself with sound design principles and software used in the industry, such as digital audio workstations (DAWs) and middleware tools. Building a portfolio of your sound design work, including original compositions and sound effects, will help you stand out to potential employers.

Conclusion

The gaming industry offers a wide array of alternative career paths for individuals with a passion for games. Whether you're interested in game journalism, marketing and PR, game testing, localization, or sound design, there are opportunities to carve out a successful career in the gaming industry. Pursuing these alternative paths can provide unique and fulfilling experiences while still allowing you to be part of the vibrant and dynamic world of gaming. The key is to follow your passion, gain relevant skills and experience, and continuously seek opportunities to grow and learn within your chosen career path.

Chapter 37: Continuing Education and Professional Development

Continuing education and professional development are key components for success in any industry, and the video game industry is no exception. As technology advances and new trends emerge, staying updated and continuously learning is essential to stay competitive and relevant in the gaming industry.

The Importance of Continuing Education

Continuing education allows individuals to expand their knowledge and skills, keeping up with the latest advancements and industry best practices. In the fast-paced world of video games, where technology is constantly evolving, it is crucial to stay current to deliver high-quality and innovative gaming experiences. By investing time and effort into continuing education, you can gain a competitive edge, enhance your career prospects, and increase your value as a professional. It demonstrates your commitment to growth and improvement, showing potential employers and clients that you are dedicated to staying at the forefront of the industry.

Professional Development Opportunities

There are various avenues for continuing education and professional development in the video game industry. Here are some key avenues to consider:

Industry Conferences and Events:

Attending industry conferences and events is an excellent way to learn from industry experts, network with professionals, and stay updated on the latest trends and advancements. Events such as the Game Developers Conference (GDC), PAX, and E3 offer valuable learning and networking opportunities.

Online Courses and Tutorials:

Online platforms provide access to a wide range of courses and tutorials on game development, programming, design principles, and other relevant topics. Platforms like Udemy, Coursera, and LinkedIn Learning offer courses taught by industry professionals that you can complete at your own pace.

Workshops and Bootcamps:

Participating in workshops and bootcamps can provide hands-on training and practical experience in specific areas of game development. These intensive programs often cover topics like game design, programming, 3D modeling, and more. They offer the opportunity to work on real projects and receive guidance from industry experts.

Online Communities and Forums:

Engaging with online communities, forums, and social media groups dedicated to video game development allows you to connect with other professionals, ask questions, share knowledge, and learn from the experiences of others. Platforms like Reddit, Discord, and Unity Connect are great places to start.

Game Jams:

Participating in game jams, where developers come together to create games within a limited timeframe, can provide a hands-on learning experience. Game jams foster creativity, problem-solving skills, and collaboration, helping you improve your game development skills while working under time pressure.

Mentorship and Networking:

Seeking mentorship from experienced professionals in the industry can offer valuable guidance and support. Networking with industry peers and attending meetups can also open doors to new opportunities and provide valuable insights and advice.

Continuously Improving Your Skills

In addition to taking advantage of continuing education opportunities, there are other ways to continuously improve your skills and stay updated in the video game industry. These include:

Following Industry Trends:

Stay informed about the latest developments, technologies, and trends in the gaming industry. Read industry publications, blogs, and news sites to stay in the loop and anticipate upcoming changes.

Experimenting and Prototyping:

Continuously experiment with new technologies, tools, and ideas. Practice prototyping to test out different concepts and game mechanics. This hands-on approach allows you to learn through trial and error and discover new ways to enhance your skills.

Reading Books and Research Papers:

Books and research papers can provide in-depth knowledge and insights into various aspects of game development. They can help you gain a deeper understanding of specific topics and expand your expertise.

Joining Game Jams and Hackathons:

Participating in game jams and hackathons not only provides an opportunity to apply your skills but also encourages collaboration and problem-solving. These events can lead to new ideas and help you explore different aspects of game development.

Engaging in Open Source Projects:

Contributing to open source projects and collaborating with other developers can broaden your skillset and expose you to different approaches and methodologies. It allows you to learn from experienced professionals and grow as a developer.

The Benefits of Continuing Education

Continuing education and professional development offer numerous benefits to individuals pursuing a career in the video game industry. These benefits include: - Increased knowledge and skills: Continuing education allows you to expand your knowledge and skills, making you a more versatile and valuable professional in the industry. - Enhanced career prospects: By staying updated and continuously learning, you improve your chances of securing job opportunities and advancing in your career. - Networking opportunities: Professional development activities provide opportunities to connect with industry peers, mentors, and potential employers, expanding your professional network. - Adaptability to industry changes: The gaming industry is ever-evolving, and by continuously learning, you can adapt to changes and remain relevant amidst technological advancements. - Personal growth: Continuing education not only enhances your professional skills but also contributes to personal growth and fulfillment. It allows you to pursue your passion and stay engaged in the industry you love.

Conclusion

Continuing education and professional development play a vital role in the video game industry. Through attending conferences, taking online courses, participating in workshops, and engaging with online communities, you can stay updated on industry trends, expand your skills, and gain a competitive edge. By continuously improving and learning, you can unlock new opportunities and carve out a successful career in the exciting world of video games.

Chapter 38: Staying Competitive in the Fast-Paced Gaming Industry

In an industry as rapidly evolving as the video game industry, staying competitive is essential for success. With new technologies, trends, and competitors emerging constantly, it is crucial for young adults pursuing a career in the gaming industry to keep up with the fast-paced nature of the field.

Continuous Learning and Development

One of the key aspects of staying competitive in the gaming industry is embracing continuous learning and development. This means regularly updating your skills, keeping up with industry trends and advancements, and seeking out new opportunities for growth. There are various ways to continue learning and developing your skills in the gaming industry. Online courses, tutorials, and forums provide a wealth of information on topics such as new game development technologies, programming languages, design principles, and marketing strategies. It is important to dedicate time to self-study and exploration, always seeking to expand your knowledge and proficiency in relevant areas.

Networking and Collaboration

Networking and collaboration are essential components of staying competitive in the gaming industry. Building a strong network of industry professionals allows you to stay informed about new opportunities, trends, and advancements. Attending conferences, industry events, and meetups can provide invaluable networking opportunities where you can connect with others in the industry. Collaborating with others on game projects or joining a development team can also enhance your competitiveness. Working with diverse teams exposes you to different perspectives and allows you to learn from others' expertise. Collaborative projects can broaden your skill set and give you the chance to showcase your abilities to potential employers or clients.

Adaptability and Flexibility

The gaming industry is known for its rapid changes and unpredictability. To stay competitive, it is crucial to be adaptable and flexible in your approach. This means being open to learning new technologies, exploring different genres or platforms, and adapting to emerging trends. Being adaptable also includes being open to new opportunities and taking risks. The gaming industry is constantly evolving, and being willing to step outside your comfort zone can lead to new and exciting career paths. Embrace change and be willing to pivot your career path if necessary.

Building a Strong Personal Brand

In a competitive industry like gaming, establishing a strong personal brand is essential. Your personal brand is your reputation, your unique selling point, and what sets you apart from other professionals. Building a strong personal brand involves showcasing your skills, passion, and unique perspective in the industry. One way to build your personal brand is through creating and sharing your own game projects. These projects can serve as showcases of your skills and creativity, demonstrating your ability to bring unique ideas to life. Using social media platforms and online portfolios, you can share your projects and engage with the gaming community, building a following and attracting the attention of potential employers or clients.

Embracing the Indie Game Scene

The indie game scene has gained significant traction in recent years, providing an avenue for independent developers to make their mark in the gaming industry. Embracing the indie game scene can be a way to stay competitive by showcasing your creativity, experimentation, and ability to stand out in a crowded market. Consider participating in game jams, where developers create games within a short timeframe. These events not only serve as great learning experiences but also provide opportunities to gain exposure and recognition in the industry. Additionally, submitting your games to indie game festivals and competitions can help you gain visibility and connect with potential collaborators or publishers.

Conclusion

Staying competitive in the fast-paced gaming industry requires continuous learning, networking, adaptability, and building a strong personal brand. By embracing these strategies, young adults pursuing a career in the gaming industry can position themselves for success and stand out in a competitive market. Always stay curious, stay connected, and stay committed to your growth and development as a video game professional.

Chapter 39: The Future of Video Game Industry

The video game industry has come a long way since its inception, and it continues to grow and evolve at an unprecedented pace. As technology advances and consumer demands change, the future of the video game industry holds exciting possibilities and challenges. In this chapter, we will explore some key trends and predictions for the future of the industry.

The Rise of Virtual Reality and Augmented Reality

Virtual reality (VR) and augmented reality (AR) have the potential to revolutionize the gaming experience. VR technology immerses players in a virtual world, providing a level of immersion and interactivity like never before. AR, on the other hand, overlays digital content onto the real world, creating a blended experience. Both VR and AR have already gained traction in the gaming industry, with devices like Oculus Rift and HTC Vive leading the way in VR, and games like Pokémon Go showcasing the potential of AR. As technology continues to improve and become more accessible, we can expect to see more games and experiences that seamlessly integrate VR and AR elements.

The Influence of Artificial Intelligence

Artificial intelligence (AI) has been steadily making its mark in the gaming industry, powering everything from intelligent NPCs (non-player characters) to sophisticated enemy behavior and procedural generation of game content. AI has the potential to enhance player experiences by creating dynamic and adaptive gameplay that responds to individual player preferences and skill levels. In the future, we can expect AI to play an even more significant role in game development. AI-driven algorithms could generate unique and personalized game narratives, adapt game difficulty in real-time, and create lifelike and believable virtual characters. This would result in games that offer highly immersive and engaging experiences tailored to each player.

Cloud Gaming and Streaming Services

Cloud gaming and streaming services have been gaining momentum in recent years, and their popularity is expected to continue growing in the future. With the advancement of internet speeds and the ubiquity of high-speed internet access, cloud gaming allows players to stream games directly to their devices without the need for powerful hardware. With cloud gaming, players can enjoy high-quality gaming experiences on a variety of devices, including smartphones, tablets, and smart TVs. This technology eliminates the need for expensive gaming consoles or gaming PCs, making gaming more accessible to a wider audience.

Continued Expansion of Mobile Gaming

Mobile gaming has already become a dominant force in the gaming industry, and its influence is only set to increase in the future. With the ubiquity of smartphones and tablets, more and more people are turning to mobile devices for their gaming needs. In the future, we can expect to see more complex and visually stunning games developed specifically for mobile platforms. The widespread adoption of 5G technology will also enable faster download and streaming speeds, further enhancing the mobile gaming experience. Additionally, the integration of augmented reality technology on mobile devices will open up new avenues for immersive gaming experiences.

The Importance of Diversity and Inclusion

The gaming industry has made significant strides in terms of diversity and inclusion in recent years, but there is still work to be done. The future of the industry demands a greater emphasis on representation and inclusivity. We can expect to see more diverse characters and narratives in games, as well as a greater push for diversity in game development teams. Additionally, accessibility features for players with disabilities will become more prevalent, ensuring that gaming experiences are inclusive for all.

Conclusion

The future of the video game industry is bright and promising. With advancements in technology, the rise of VR and AR, the influence of AI, the growth of cloud gaming, the expansion of mobile gaming, and a greater focus on diversity and inclusion, the industry is poised to continue captivating audiences and pushing the boundaries of interactive entertainment. It is an exciting time for young adults pursuing a career in the video game industry, as they will play a pivotal role in shaping the future of gaming.

Chapter 40: Your Journey Begins Here

Congratulations! You've reached the final chapter of "Ctrl+Alt+Achieve: A Roadmap for Young Adults Pursuing the Video Game Industry." Throughout this book, we have explored various aspects of the video game industry, from understanding its history and different sectors to mastering game design principles and exploring alternative career paths. Now, it's time to embark on your own journey in the exciting world of video game development. This chapter marks the beginning of your personal exploration and implementation of everything you have learned so far. It is where you take the reins and start making your dreams a reality. Your journey begins here, but remember that this is just the beginning, and there is a whole world of possibilities waiting for you.

Setting Clear Goals

As you start your journey, it is crucial to set clear goals for yourself. What do you want to achieve in the video game industry? Do you want to become a game designer, programmer, sound designer, or explore another niche? Take the time to reflect on your passions and interests, and then set specific, measurable, achievable, relevant, and time-bound (SMART) goals. Setting clear goals will help you stay focused and motivated throughout your journey.

Continuous Learning

The video game industry is constantly evolving, with new technologies, trends, and techniques emerging regularly. To stay competitive and relevant, it is essential to embrace a mindset of continuous learning. Seek out opportunities to expand your knowledge and skills, whether through online courses, workshops, conferences, or simply experimenting with new tools and technologies. Be open to feedback and always strive to improve yourself as a game industry professional.

Building a Network

Networking is a vital aspect of the video game industry. Building connections with other professionals, peers, and potential employers can open doors to new opportunities and collaborations. Attend industry events, join online communities and forums, and utilize professional social networking platforms like LinkedIn to connect with others in the gaming industry. Engage in meaningful conversations, share your work, and foster relationships that can benefit you throughout your career.

Building Your Portfolio

Throughout this book, we have emphasized the importance of building a strong portfolio. Now is the time to curate and showcase your best work. Include projects that highlight your skills and demonstrate your creativity and problem-solving abilities. Don't be afraid to think outside the box and showcase your unique style and ideas. Your portfolio will be a key tool for impressing potential employers or clients, so take the time to present your work in a visually appealing and organized manner.

Applying for Internships and Entry-Level Positions

Internships and entry-level positions are valuable stepping stones in your journey towards a successful career in the video game industry. They provide hands-on experience, exposure to real projects, and the opportunity to work alongside industry professionals. Research and apply for internships or entry-level positions that align with your goals and interests. Remember, even if you don't land your dream job right away, every opportunity can contribute to your growth and development.

Being Resilient

The journey to a career in the video game industry may not always be smooth sailing. Rejections, setbacks, and challenges are inevitable. It's important to develop resilience and perseverance. Don't let failures deter you. Learn from them, adapt, and keep pushing forward. The most successful professionals in the industry have faced obstacles but persisted despite them. Believe in your abilities and stay committed to your goals.

Embracing the Passion

Lastly, as you embark on your journey in the video game industry, don't forget the fuel that drives it all – passion. Remember why you chose this path and let that passion shine through in every project you undertake. The video game industry is fueled by creative minds who have a genuine love for games and the desire to create immersive experiences for players. Embrace your passion, stay curious, and continue to create and innovate. Your journey begins here, but it doesn't end with this book. It is an ongoing adventure filled with discovery, growth, and endless possibilities. So, take what you have learned and start forging your own path in the captivating world of video game development. Remember, with dedication, perseverance, and a passion for games, you have the potential to achieve great things. Good luck, and may your journey be filled with success and fulfillment!

careers in screen·ie/role/fx-artist/

screenskills.com

Printed in Great Britain
by Amazon